CHAUCER

CHAUCER

BY

ALFRED W. POLLARD
GENERAL EDITOR OF THE 'GLOBE CHAUCER'

GREENWOOD PRESS, PUBLISHERS
NEW YORK

Originally published in 1931
by Macmillan and Co., London

First Greenwood Reprinting 1969

Library of Congress Catalogue Card Number 69-14038

SBN 8371-1856-5

PRINTED IN UNITED STATES OF AMERICA

CONTENTS

INTRODUCTION

IN 1893 when this little book was first published it opened
with the remark that the fame of Chaucer had triumphed
over many obstacles. For nearly four centuries after his
death his poems were so imperfectly transcribed and
printed that he who hardly ever wrote a bad line, and
whose music and mastery of words are almost unrivalled,
was apologised for as some rude rhymer. His works were
praised for their "learning", printed in black letter as an
antiquarian curiosity, paraphrased and translated till he
could not himself have recognised them. And yet through
all this his fame survived. For in his works, as nowhere
else, men found the colour and life of an earlier day. He
stood at the close of the Middle Ages and illustrated their
ideals and their practice, their religion and their per-
plexities: chivalry and satire, cynicism and simplicity
met together in his verse. Yet a greater gift he had given
his readers, a gallery of portraits more numerous and
more vividly sketched than can be found in any other
writer of English, save only Shakespeare and Scott. When
all his art was obscured by the imperfection of the current
text, even for his matter only it is little to be wondered
at that men had been found to praise him in almost every
decade since his death. At last, in 1737, the tide of degrada-
tion was turned by T. Morrell's edition of the Prologue
and Knight's Tale. This, though accompanied by modern-
ised versions, gave (with collations and illustrative notes)
a text which allowed much more of the poet's music to be

heard. The first scholarly edition of all the *Canterbury Tales* was issued by Thomas Tyrwhitt in 1775–78. Other editions followed, but no great step forward was made till, in 1868, a Chaucer Society was founded by Frederick James Furnivall, which printed the best manuscripts, rejected unauthentic pieces included in the old editions, and replaced the imaginative early biographies from researches mainly at the Record Office. This little primer of 1893 was an attempt to epitomise the results of the work of the Society. In the same year there came William Morris's magnificently printed, decorated, and illustrated Kelmscott *Chaucer*, in 1894 the first volume of Walter Skeat's richly annotated Oxford text, and in 1898 the "Globe" edition, of which Furnivall became the dedicatee instead of, as he should have been, the editor. After Skeat's great edition research work by English students slackened, but the quest was continued by American workers with excellent results, to incorporate some of which (notably those of Professors Emerson, Kittredge, Livingston Lowes, Manly, and Edith Rickert, and the Danish Professor Brusendorff) is the main business of this revision. In 1893 it was claimed that Chaucer had more readers and lovers than ever before. This is still more true in the present day.

CHAPTER I

CHAUCER, THE KING'S SERVANT

§ 1. **The Name Chaucer.**—The name Chaucer is believed to have become quite extinct, but in the thirteenth and fourteenth centuries it occurs not unfrequently. From the year 1226 downwards we have a chain of London Chaucers; from 1272 Chaucers are met with in different parts of the eastern counties. The name, which means *shoemaker*, is likely to have cropped up in many places.

We cannot, therefore, assume that any particular Chaucer
we find mentioned is a kinsman of the poet; we cannot
even be absolutely sure that we may not sometimes be
confusing two Chaucers, with the same Christian name,
who were really distinct. We have no reason to believe
that this has actually happened, but the possibility may
serve to show with how much difficulty our scanty records
of the poet's life have been pieced together.

§ 2. **The Poet's Parentage.**—The first Chaucer with
whom we are concerned held, at the time of his death, a
small property in Ipswich of the annual value of twenty
shillings or thereabouts, *i.e.* some £30 of our post-war
money. In 1310 he had been appointed one of the col-
lectors in the Port of London of the new customs upon
wine granted by the merchants of Aquitaine. This Robert
le Chaucer was the poet's grandfather. His wife, Mary
(who had previously married one Heyroun), may possibly
have been by birth a Stace. Their son's name was John.
On her second husband's death Mary married yet again,
apparently one of Robert's kinsmen, a Richard le Chaucer,
who lived in the ward of Cordwanerstrete, London. On
3rd December 1324, when John Chaucer was between
twelve and fourteen years of age, Thomas Stace of Ipswich and others seized his person, with the object of
forcibly marrying him to Joan de Westhale, who had an
interest in some land in Suffolk, of which the ultimate
remainder was settled on John. Richard le Chaucer
took up his stepson's cause. Stace and his associates
were fined the heavy sum of £250 (some £7500 in post-
war value), and we learn from a subsequent plea to
Parliament for the mitigation of the penalty that in
1328 John Chaucer was still unmarried and living with
his stepfather.

§ 3. **John and Agnes Chaucer.**—Richard Chaucer was
a vintner. When he died, in 1349, he left his house and

tavern, not to his stepson—then, we may suppose, a thriving citizen—but to the Church of St. Mary Aldermary. John Chaucer also was a vintner. On 12th June 1338 a protection against being sued in his absence was granted to him with some forty-five others, who were crossing the sea with the King. Ten years later he acted as deputy to the King's Butler in the port of Southampton. He owned a house in Thames Street, London, which the poet parted with in 1382. We hear in 1349 of his wife Agnes, "niece of Hamo de Copton", an official in the Mint: she was daughter of John Copton and widow of Henry (?) de Northwell, who may have had a connection with the Court. When John Chaucer died, some time after 16th January 1366, Agnes again consoled herself, and appears in May 1367 as the wife of Bartholomew atte Chapel, another vintner. That she found a third husband so quickly in 1367 makes it probable that in 1349 she had not been married to John Chaucer for many years. But we cannot be sure that she was John's only wife, or that Geoffrey Chaucer was his son by her.

§ 4. **Chaucer's Birth.**—Geoffrey Chaucer, then, was the son of John Chaucer, citizen and vintner of London. In the absence of any evidence to the contrary it is probable that he was born in the house in Thames Street, and that his mother's name was Agnes. It is probable also that he was born about 1340, a little later rather than earlier. In October 1386, when he gave evidence in the suit between Richard, Lord Scrope, and Sir Robert Grosvenor, his age was entered as "forty years or more", a statement the value of which is diminished but not destroyed by the proved carelessness of entries as to one or two other witnesses. We have, however, absolutely no evidence of any weight in favour of any one particular year as that of the poet's birth. In such a case there is an obvious advantage in a round date, and "about" or "probably little later

than" 1340 as Chaucer's birth-year fits in very fairly well
with everything we know of his subsequent life.

§ 5. **Service in the Household of the Countess of Ulster.**
—The first certain information we have about Chaucer
is of his service in the household of Elizabeth de Burgh,
Countess of Ulster, and wife of Lionel, third son of Edward III. The fragments of her Household Accounts,
which contain the name Galfridus Chaucer, were found
appropriately enough in the covers of a manuscript containing Lydgate's *Storie of Thebes* and Hoccleve's *Rege-
ment of Princes*, so that the works of two brother poets
have helped to preserve this record of Chaucer's early life.
The accounts show that in April 1357 the Countess was
in London, and that an entire suit of clothes, consisting
of a paltock, or short cloak, a pair of red and black
breeches, and shoes, was then provided for Geoffrey
Chaucer, at a cost of seven shillings, *i.e.* about ten guineas
present value. In May of the same year another article of
clothing was purchased for him in London. In the following December, when the Countess was at her seat at Hatfield, in Yorkshire, there is an entry of two shillings and
sixpence paid to Geoffrey Chaucer "for necessaries at
Christmas". We cannot tell whether the smallness of
these sums as compared with other payments was due to
Chaucer's youth or to his holding an inferior position in
the Countess's household.

These three entries are the only ones which refer
directly to Chaucer, but we learn from others that the
Countess took part in several great festivities at Court,
and at these the poet may have been present. We learn,
too, that the winter months of each year were mostly
spent at Hatfield, in Yorkshire, and that towards the end
of 1357 the Countess of Ulster entertained at Hatfield her
brother-in-law, John of Gaunt, afterwards the poet's best
patron. In addition to this training in Court life we learn

from a statement by "Master Buckley", a sixteenth-century custodian of the records of the Inner Temple, that Chaucer was entered as fined for beating a Franciscan friar in Fleet Street, that he was thus at some uncertain date a student there and would have received instruction not only in law, but in history, music, dancing, and other accomplishments useful for a career in the King's service, for which it would thus seem that he was definitely prepared.

§ 6. **Chaucer's Campaign in France.**—The Scrope suit in which Chaucer, as we have seen, was called on to give evidence in 1386, related to the right to bear a certain coat of arms. In the record of the trial Chaucer is entered as having himself borne arms for twenty-seven years, *i.e.* since 1359, and his testimony refers to the unlucky campaign in France of that year, during which, he declared, when before the town of "Retters" (probably Réthel, not far from Rheims), he had constantly seen Henry le Scrope armed in a certain manner, until he himself was taken prisoner. His imprisonment did not last long, as on 1st March 1360 the King contributed no less than £16 (£480 present value) to his ransom. Even if the King's contribution constituted the whole ransom, this was a large sum, but Chaucer probably went to the war in the suite of Prince Lionel, or of the King himself, and this may have increased the price set upon his liberty.

§ 7. **He becomes a Yeoman of the King's Chamber.**— In the autumn of 1360 Chaucer is found acting as a King's messenger, bearing letters from Calais, where peace with France was being negotiated. He may have entered the King's household while still studying at the Inner Temple; all we know is that on 20th June 1367, for past and future services, Edward III. granted him a pension, or annual salary, of 20 marks (£13 : 6 : 8, nearly £400 present value) for life, under the title *dilectus valettus noster*. Chaucer was thus one of the yeomen of the King's chamber, a position which in a year or two improved into that of an *armiger, scutifer*, or squire.

§ 8. **His supposed Love Suit.**—At the close of this period, during the greater part of which we are thus ignorant of his doings, Chaucer composed his *Book of the Duchesse*, an allegorical lament for the death, in 1369, of Blanche of Lancaster, the wife of John of Gaunt. It is usually maintained also that before 1369 (possibly before 1366) he had written the *Compleynt unto Pite*, which, if so, is the earliest of his original poems which has come down to us. The *Compleynt* is a beautiful little poem, of which it is impossible to say whether the motive was merely fanciful or had some real foundation in Chaucer's own life. He was about, he says, to complain to Pity against the cruelty of Love, who tortured him for his faith; but when after many years, during which he had ever sought a time to speak, "al bespreynt with teres", he ran to Pity, he found her dead, buried in his lady's heart, and so his "bill" or petition was unavailing.

The same tone of melancholy pervades the poem to the *Book of the Duchesse*. Sorrowful imagination is always wholly in the poet's mind, he is a mazed thing, "alway in point to falle adoun", living in melancholy and fear of death, with all his spirits crushed by heaviness and lack of sleep.

> But men might axĕ me, why so
> I may not slepe, and what me is?
> But nathĕles, who askĕ this
> Leseth his asking trewĕly.
> Myselven can not tellĕ why
> The soth; but trewely, as I gesse,
> I holde hit be a siknesse
> That I have suffred this eight yere,
> And yet my bote is never the nere;
> For ther is phisicien but oon
> That may me hele; but that is doon.
> Passe we over, until eft;
> That wil not be moot nede be left.

The allusions in these two poems certainly point to an unrequited love. The reality of the love is another matter. Many poets before now have feigned passions which had no serious part in their lives, but were recognised on both sides as a pretty amusement, conferring some distinction on the lady, and supplying the poet with a convenient peg on which to hang love verses. In the days of chivalry knights might devote their lances and poets their song to their ladies' service without hope of any other reward than a smile, and it was maintained that marriage with another was no bar to the continuance of this honourable service. We must, therefore, be on our guard against taking Chaucer's mysterious and unhappy love too literally. At one time the importance of these allusions was very greatly exaggerated, so that they were even held to raise difficulties as to the date of the poet's marriage.

§ 9. **Chaucer's Marriage.**—On 12th September 1366 a Philippa Chaucer was in the service of the Queen, and was granted a pension of ten marks yearly for life. We know that this Philippa Chaucer in 1374, and occasionally in subsequent years, received part of her pension by the hands of Geoffrey Chaucer, her husband. That she was called in the grant *una Domicellarum Camerae Reginae*, "one of the damoiselles of the Queen's chamber", does not affect the probability that Philippa was the poet's wife as early as 1366. The term *domicella* referred to the office or rank Philippa held, and could be applied to a married woman as well as to a girl. It is even said that it was customary for these damoiselles of the chamber to be married. Except the poetical allusions to another love, we have no reason for postponing Chaucer's marriage save the fact that on 30th August 1372 John of Gaunt had given Philippa Chaucer a pension of £10, and that on 13th June 1374 a pension of this same sum was granted by the Duke to Chaucer and his wife for good services rendered by them "to the said Duke, his Consort and his mother the Queen". It is maintained that this was only a re-grant of Philippa's former pension, and that the cause of the re-grant must be that between 1372 and 1374 "the cousins or namesakes", Geoffrey Chaucer and Philippa Chaucer, had become man and wife. Marriage between cousins in the fourteenth century required a papal dispensation, and the "namesake" theory is too easy a way out of the difficulty to be satisfactory. It seems best to believe that when Philippa Chaucer was granted her pension in September 1366 she was already the poet's wife. If so, we must not take the allusions quoted above too seriously.

§ 10. **Philippa and Thomas Chaucer.**— If Philippa Chaucer was not the poet's "cousin or namesake", who was she? A slender chain of evidence suggests the answer Philippa Roet, daughter of Sir Payne Roet of Hainault, and sister of Katharine Roet, who, after the death of her husband, Sir Hugh Swynford, became the third wife of John of Gaunt, in whose family she had been governess. In the beginning of the fifteenth century a certain Thomas Chaucer was a man of great importance, and it has been frequently conjectured that he was Geoffrey Chaucer's son, a connection which is asserted as a fact by Thomas Gascoigne, Chancellor of the University of Oxford (died 1458). Gascoigne's assertion has received some slight corroboration from a discovery that from 1390–91 onwards a Geoffrey Chaucer, possibly the poet (for the appointment was in the gift of descendants of his first patroness, the Countess of Ulster), held the Forestership of North Petherton, Somerset, and that in 1416–17 a Thomas Chaucer was granted the same post. But we have no proof of the identity of these two Chaucers, so that, as has been said, the corroboration thus offered is only slight. We know, however, that the important Thomas

Chaucer was in great favour with the Lancastrian kings
(young Prince Hal even calling him his "cousin"), and we
know, too, that towards the close of his life he exchanged
the Chaucer arms for those of Roet. Thus his descent from
Sir Payne Roet appears not unlikely, and it is certainly
possible that this descent was through Philippa Chaucer.
The connection which would thus be established between
the poet and John of Gaunt would explain the many marks
of favour which the latter bestowed upon Chaucer and
his wife, but the question has very little bearing upon
Chaucer's poetry, and may well be regarded as an open
one. If Chaucer's wife was Philippa Roet, the poet was
most likely the father of the Elizabeth Chaucer, for whose
novitiate at the Abbey of Barking John of Gaunt paid a
considerable sum in 1381. But the only child of his of
whom we have certain knowledge is the little Lewis for
whom he compiled a treatise on the Astrolabe, calculated
for the year 1391, when the boy was ten years old.

§ 11. **Chaucer's Life at Court.**—We left Chaucer as a
valet or yeoman of the King's chamber, shortly on the
point of being promoted to the rank of an esquire.[1] As a
valet his duties would be to serve in the chamber, make
beds, hold and carry torches, and do "divers other things",
which the King or the chamberlain might command him.
He would eat in the chamber before the King, and have
an allowance of food and beer, and every year a robe in
cloth or a mark in money, and three shillings and fourpence twice a year for shoes. If sent out of the Court on
the King's business, fourpence a day was allowed for expenses. By Christmas 1368 Chaucer had risen to be an
"Esquire of less degree", receiving sevenpence-halfpenny
a day, and two robes yearly, or forty shillings in their

[1] These details are gleaned from the Household Books of Edward II.
and Edward IV. (*Ch. Soc.*), between which there are fewer variations
than might be expected.

stead. We do not know exactly what were the duties of
the esquires (there were thirty-seven of them in 1368);
but an old manuscript tells us that "these Esquires of
household of old be accustomed, winter and summer, in
afternoons and in evenings, to draw to Lords chambers
within Court, there to keep honest company after their
cunning, in talking of chronicles of Kings, and of other
policies, or in piping or harping, 'songinges' or other 'acts
marcealls', to help to occupy the Court, and accompany
strangers, till the time require of departing". If such tasks
formed an important part of the esquire's work, no
wonder that Chaucer soon rose in favour.

§ 12. **His Diplomatic Missions—First Visit to Italy.**—
On 17th July 1368 Chaucer, for what purpose is unknown,
was granted leave to cross the sea from Dover with two
hackneys, twenty shillings for expenses and ten pounds
in letters of exchange. In 1369 he took part in the war in
France. In 1370 he was abroad on the King's service, and
obtained letters of protection from creditors till Michael-
mas, when he returned and received his pension on 8th
October. He received his pension with his own hands in
1371 and 1372, but we know nothing of his doings until
12th November of the latter year, when he was joined in
a commission with two citizens of Genoa to treat with the
Duke, citizens, and merchants of that place for the choice
of some port in England where Genoese merchants might
settle and trade. For his expenses he was allowed an
advance of a hundred marks, and a further sum of thirty-
eight marks was paid after his return to London, which
took place, we are explicitly told, on 23rd May 1373.

As we shall see in another chapter, Chaucer was very
greatly influenced by the writings of Dante, Petrarch,
and Boccaccio, and borrowed a little from the first and
second, and a great deal from the third. It is impossible
to date this intimate acquaintance with Italian literature

from any earlier time than the Genoese mission of 1372–
1373. The King's esquire may very probably have learned
to speak Italian, and been chosen for the mission for this
very reason. But none of his contemporaries show any
trace of direct Italian influence, and it is unlikely that
previously to his mission Chaucer would have had much
access to Italian manuscripts, which, on the other hand,
could be easily purchased either on this or on his subsequent stay in Italy. This first visit was not confined to
Genoa, but extended also, so the warrant of repayment
tells us, to Florence. If we can believe that Chaucer also
visited Padua (some distance off), we may take as apply-
ing literally to the poet himself the statement of his
imaginary Clerk of Oxenford that the tale of the patience
of Grisilde was "lerned at Padowe of a worthy clerk . . .
Fraunceys Petrark, the laureat poete". For Petrarch
was at Padua from November 1372 to September 1373
and was then engaged on the Latin version of the story
of Grisilde, which Chaucer undoubtedly used for his
translation. At the least there is no impossibility in this
meeting between the two great poets, and it is pleasant
to imagine it (see also § 46).

§ 13. **Comptrollership of the Customs.**—From the
mission to Genoa dates a great advance in Chaucer's
prosperity. On St. George's Day 1374 the King, then at
Windsor, granted him a pitcher of wine daily, commuted
for a money payment in 1377 and in 1378 for a pension
of twenty marks. In May he leased from the Corporation
of London the dwelling-house over the gate of Aldgate.
In June he was appointed, at a salary of £10, Comptroller
of the Customs and Subsidy of Wools, Skins, and Tanned
Hides in the Port of London, with the obligation to write
the rolls of his office with his own hand, and to be con-
tinually present. In the same month he was granted by
John of Gaunt the pension of £10 for the service rendered

by him and his wife Philippa, which we have already
noticed in § 9. In 1375 two wardships were granted him,
one of which, that of Edward Staplegate of Kent, subsequently brought him in £104. In 1376 the King made him
a grant of £71 : 4 : 6, the price of some wool forfeited at
the Customs for non-payment of duty; and just before
Christmas he receives ten marks as his wages as one of
the retinue of Sir John Burley in some secret service. In
February 1377 he went to Flanders with Sir Thomas
Percy on a secret mission, and subsequently was engaged
in France, probably in connection with the negotiations
for peace. Perhaps because of these absences he was
allowed to exercise his Comptrollership by deputy.

§ 14. **Second Mission to Italy.**—On 21st June 1377
Edward III. died, but the advisers of the eleven-year-old
Richard II. were favourable to Chaucer, and the change
of kings only increased his prosperity. Early in the next
year he probably took part in another embassy to France,
to negotiate Richard's marriage with a daughter of the
French King, and in the following May we find him pre-
paring to go with Sir Edward Berkeley on a mission to
Lombardy, there to treat on military matters with
Bernabo Visconti, Lord of Milan (whose imprisonment
and death form one of the tragedies of his Monk's Tale),
and with the famous free-lance, Sir John Hawkwood.
He obtained the usual letters of protection, and appointed
two friends, Richard Forrester and the poet Gower, his
agents during his absence. The arrears of his pension
(£20), with an advance of two marks on the current
quarter, were paid him, and on 28th May he received one
hundred marks for his wages and expenses during his
mission. Of the mission itself we know nothing, but
Chaucer must have got through his business quickly,
since he returned to London on 19th September, his total
expenses amounting to £80 : 13 : 4. As far as we know,

with this journey to Lombardy Chaucer's career as a
diplomatist came to an end, and for the next year or
two he had no relief from the drudgery of his clerk's work
at the Customs. All his employments were, no doubt,
helpful to him as a poet in widening his knowledge of
men and places, but the two missions, 1st December 1372
to 23rd May 1373 and 28th May to 19th September 1378,
during which he must have spent at least several months
in Italy, had probably an influence on his poetry greater
than any other event in his life.

§ 15. **Work in London and Loss of Office.**—For the next
five years or so we must picture Chaucer as attending to
his duties as Comptroller of the Customs and Subsidies
(§ 13), receiving his own and his wife's pensions at ir-
regular intervals, and probably dunning the Treasury for
£22 due to him for his last French mission until in March
1381 it was finally paid. On three successive New Year's
Days (1380–82) his wife was presented with a silver-gilt
cup and cover by the Duke of Lancaster, and in May 1382
Chaucer himself was appointed Comptroller also of the
Petty Customs of the Port of London, with leave to
exercise his office by deputy. In February 1385 he was
allowed to appoint a permanent deputy for his old Comptrollership and in October was appointed a Justice of the
Peace for Kent. In the following April he possibly took
advantage of his new leisure to go on the merry pilgrimage to Canterbury, his glorified version of which has ever
been accounted his chief title to fame. From 1st October
to 1st November 1386 he sat in the Parliament at Westminster as one of the Knights of the Shire for Kent, and
on 15th October gave evidence, as we have seen, in the
Scrope case (§ 6). But his hitherto unbroken good fortune
was now interrupted. His patron, John of Gaunt, was
superseded in the government by the Duke of Gloucester,
and a commission was appointed for inquiring into the

state of the Subsidies and Customs, with the result that we hear of the nomination in December of successors to Chaucer in both his Comptrollerships. He had exercised them for some time through a deputy, but it is more probable that he was superseded as a follower of the Duke of Lancaster than for any irregularities connected with his own work. Shortly before this he must have given up his house in Aldgate, for in October of this year it was let to another tenant, and we have no knowledge where the poet lived during the next thirteen years.

§ 16. **Chaucer's Married Life.**—On 1st May 1380 a certain Cecilia de Chaumpaigne executed an absolute release to Chaucer from all liability *de meo raptu*. No compensation is mentioned as having been offered by the poet, and in the view of the present writer the most probable interpretation of this release points to Chaucer having been accessory in some such attempt on Cecilia Chaumpaigne as the Staces had practised against his own father. His wife probably died shortly after midsummer 1387, as her pension was then paid for the last time, and on 5th July Chaucer took steps to go for a year to Calais. We know really nothing about the marriage, but it has generally been assumed that it was an unhappy one. Chaucer's own experience certainly did not prevent him from following the mediaeval satirists in their gibes at the married state and scant respect for wives, and in the envoy to the Clerk's Tale and the *Envoy to Bukton* he assumes an attitude of intense bitterness, whether in jest or earnest can hardly be decided. It is noteworthy, however, that in the poems which we know to have been written during his wife's lifetime this bitterness against marriage does not appear. The worst that can be alleged against him up to the beginning of the *Canterbury Tales* (1387?) is that in the *Hous of Fame* he alludes to a voice—supposed to be his wife's—bidding him *Awake* of a morning in ungoodly

tones, a jest which heavy sleepers who share the poet's
objection to being roused will not be inclined to take
seriously. As far as the evidence of his poems goes—and
we have really nothing else to guide us—Chaucer was a
less religious and a less clean-spoken man when his wife's
influence was removed than he had been during her
life.

§ 17. **Financial Troubles—New Employments.**—As we
have seen, Philippa Chaucer's pension died with her, and
the loss of this and of his employment may have reduced
the poet to some straits, and even be connected with his
obtaining on 8th July protection for a year against being
sued in his absence while at Calais with his friend Sir
William Beauchamp, captain of the town. In November
and December he received payments personally in
London; in April and again in June 1388 writs were
issued against him, and in May he assigned his two pensions of twenty marks each from Edward III. to a certain
John Scalby, presumably for cash. Better times, however,
were approaching. In May 1389 the King, now twenty-two,
took the reins in his own hands. The Duke of Gloucester
retired to the country, and John of Gaunt was once more
in favour. On the following 12th July Chaucer reaped the
benefit of these changes, being appointed Clerk of the
King's Works at the Palace of Westminster, the Tower of
London, and various royal manors, at a salary of two
shillings a day, and with power to employ a deputy. A
year later he was ordered to procure workmen and
materials for the repair of St. George's Chapel, Windsor,
and was paid the costs of putting up scaffolds in Smithfield
for the King and Queen to see the jousts in May. In the
intervening March he had been named, with five others,
as a commissioner for the repairs of the roadways on the
banks of the river between Greenwich and Woolwich. It
was about this time also, between June 1390 and June

1391, that he may have been appointed Forester to North Petherton Park, in Somersetshire (see § 10); but by the summer of the year 1391 he had lost both his lucrative clerkships, though he received various payments in connection with them as late as 1393.

It was during this brief spell of renewed prosperity that Chaucer endured the unpleasant experience of being robbed twice in one day (6th September 1390) by members of the same gang of highwaymen—the first time at Westminster of £10, the second at Hatcham, by the "foul oak", of £9 : 3 : 8. The money was not his own, but the King's, and was forgiven him by writ on 6th January 1391. One of the gang turned "approver" or informer against the rest; but being challenged to a wager by battle and defeated, was himself hanged, a fate which seems eventually to have befallen most of his comrades.

§ 18. **Last Years and Death.**—Having parted with his pensions and lost his clerkships, Chaucer had no means of subsistence, *i.e.* none known to us, save his possible Forestership at North Petherton and the Commissionership of the Roadways between Greenwich and Woolwich. From one of these latter places, "forgete in solitary wilderness", he wrote to his friend Scogan, a witty fellow "at the stremès hede Of grace, of alle honour and of worthynesse", *i.e.* the Court at Windsor, a humorous poem on Scogan's having bid farewell to love. The last verse, in which he contrasts their fortunes rather sadly, contains the petition, "myndè thy friend there it may fructify". It is possible, therefore, that it may have been through Scogan's good offices that in 1394 Richard II. came to Chaucer's relief with a grant of a new pension of £20 a year for life. It is probable, however, that the poet still found it difficult to make both ends meet, for during the next few years we find him frequently obtaining loans from the Exchequer in advance of his pension, though some of these may betoken only that he was short of coined money. In May 1398 he obtained from the King letters of protection against enemies suing him—not a certain, but a probable sign of poverty—for we know that just at this time he was being sued for a debt of a little over £14. In October of the same year Richard granted him a tun of wine yearly, in answer to a petition which seems to have begged it, somewhat pitifully, "for the sake of God and as a work of charity". A few months later the King himself was deposed.

Richard II. had turned no deaf ear to Chaucer's appeals, but on the new king his claims as an old adherent of John of Gaunt were still stronger. A poem entitled a *Compleynt to his Purs*, addressed to Henry IV., elicited a fresh pension of forty marks (October 1399) in addition to the £20 granted by Richard II. Curiously enough the poet lost the written grants for both these pensions, and had to apply for fresh copies of them, which were duly granted. Thus assisted, Chaucer, on 24th December, took a lease of a tenement in the garden of St. Mary's Chapel, Westminster, for fifty-three years, of which he lived for less than one. He drew an instalment of his £20 pension on 21st February 1400, and £5 more on account on 5th June, by the hands of a friend. On 25th October, just ten months after he had taken his long lease, he died, and was buried in St. Benet's Chapel, in Westminster Abbey, where his grave has since been surrounded by those of many later poets. In 1556 a pious admirer erected a tombstone of grey marble to his memory (it is from this we learn the date of his death), probably to replace an earlier one which had worn away. A stained-glass window, with portraits of the poet and his contemporaries, and views of the pilgrims setting forth and arriving at Canterbury, was placed over against his grave by Dean Stanley in 1868.

§ 19. **Summary.**—As opposed to the legends noticed in § 22 Chaucer's authentic biography has been built up mainly from entries of payments in the royal accounts and casual references in legal documents—very dull materials for a poet's life. In their sum, however, they offer a fairly detailed picture of the outward circumstances of Chaucer's life, and should correct any idea that he was the son of a retail wine-seller, picked out by some lucky chance for service at Court and making his way there mainly by his poetry and his wife's connection with John of Gaunt. The details of payments, diplomatic missions, and home appointments do not matter. What we have to remember is that Chaucer came of a well-to-do middle-class family, connected with the wine trade, the civil service and the court, and that he was probably given an expensive education at the Inner Temple to qualify him for the King's service; that, at an early age, the poet was introduced to the life of a great court; that he saw at least a little military service; that he was employed on diplomatic missions, sometimes in conjunction with men of high rank, and that as these missions were frequent, it is a fair inference that he showed unusual capacity for them; that some of these missions took him to France, where he had also endured an imprisonment of a few months, and that on two other occasions he was absent in all for nearly ten months on missions to Italy. Before these missions were over he had obtained a footing in what we may call the civil service, in which he continued, transacting business of very various kinds, for a great many years, his fortunes apparently rising and falling with those of the house of Lancaster. During a great part of this time his income must have been considerable; but it is probable that he spent it freely, and was acquainted with poverty as well as wealth. We know also that he married, and have no good reason to believe that the marriage was unhappy, though we find traces in his early poems of another and unsuccessful love.

§ 20. **Variety of Chaucer's Life.**—Chaucer was thus, at various times of his life, a courtier, soldier, diplomatist, and man of business, and it was mainly by hard work done in these various capacities that he earned his living, though in his old age the fact that he was a great poet may have won for him rather more consideration than kings always show to their worn-out servants. Probably no other poet of equal rank has ever led so active and varied a life, and it is because we find Chaucer in his poems so shrewd a man of the world, so astonishingly observant, and so good a judge of character, that we take an interest in finding out how he obtained his experience. When we come to examine his writings we shall find that the twofold life he was obliged to lead had one bad effect: it caused him to leave many of his poems unfinished. If we may take a passage in his *Hous of Fame* (Bk. ii. ll. 139-152) quite literally, he must often have been in danger of overwork, though the absolutely healthy tone of his poems forbids us to think that he ever fell a victim to it. There it is said to him:

> And noght oonly for ferre contree,
> That ther no tydynge cometh to thee,
> But of thy verray neyghèbors,
> That dwellen almoste at thy dors,
> Thou herist neyther that nor this,
> For when thy labour doon al ys,
> And hast y-made thy rekenynges,
> Insted of reste and newè thynges,
> Thou goost home to thy house anoon,
> And, al-so dombe as any stoon,
> Thou sittest at another booke,
> Tyl fully dasewyd ys thy looke,
> And lyvest thus as an heremyte,
> Although thyn abstynence ys lyte.

In the *Legende of Good Women* (ll. 29-39) there is another passage which tells in the main the same tale, but tells us, too, what it was that kept the poet so healthy-minded all his days. Here he is speaking himself:

> And as for me, though that I konne but lyte,
> On bokes for to rede I me delyte,
> And to hem give I feyth and ful credence,
> And in myn herte have hem in reverence
> So hertely, that ther is game noon
> That fro my bokes maketh me to goon,
> But yt be seldom on the holy day,
> Save, certeynly, when that the monethe of May
> Is comen, and that I here the foules synge,
> And that the floures gynnen for to sprynge,—
> Farewel my boke, and my devocioun!

§ 21. **His Person.**—Thus we see that Chaucer had the habits of a student as well as those of a man of business, and if we ask how he looked when he walked about the world, the way he is addressed in his *Canterbury Tales* (B. 1888–94) by the merry Host shows us how he himself imagined that his appearance would strike others.

> Approche neer and look up merrily.
> Now war you, sires, and lat this man have place.
> He in the waast is shape as wel as I;
> This were a popet in an arm to embrace
> For any womman, smal and fair of face.
> He semeth elvyssh by his contenance,
> For unto no wight dooth he daliance.

The best-known portrait of Chaucer is taken from the "lyknesse" in body-colour which Thomas Hoccleve caused to be painted on one of the leaves of his own *Regiment of Princes*, now the Harleian MS. 4866 in the British Museum, and usually publicly exhibited in the show-case devoted to English manuscripts. Dr. Furnivall's description and comment on it bring out its qualities so well that they are here quoted. "The face", he says, "is wise and tender, full of a sweet and kindly sadness at first sight, but with much bonhomie in it on a further look, and with deep-set, far-looking grey eyes. Not the face of a very old man, a totterer, but of one with work in him yet, looking kindly, though seriously, out on the world before him. Unluckily the parted grey moustache and the vermilion above and below the lips render it difficult to catch the expression of the mouth; but the lips seem parted, as if to speak. Two tufts of white beard are on the chin; and a fringe of white hair shows from under the black hood. One feels one would like to go to such a man when one was in trouble, and hear his wise and gentle speech." The background of the portrait is green against a brown border, the poet's dress black, relieved by the red strings by which hang his pen-case and beads. Other portraits exist, but they are less carefully drawn. They serve, however, by their general resemblance to show us that the one we owe to the piety of Hoccleve is no mere fancy sketch.

§ 22. **Chaucer Legends.**—To complete this sketch of Chaucer's life it is unhappily necessary to mention, in order that they be recognised when met with, some entirely fanciful statements about him which, until the end of the nineteenth century, disfigured most of his biographies. For many of these the imagination of the poet's first biographer, the antiquary Leland, who lived in the reign of Henry VIII., is primarily responsible, though many later writers improved on his inventions. Thus Leland's ungrounded assertions that the poet was of noble birth, was born in Oxfordshire or Berkshire, and educated at Oxford were rendered more specific by statements, equally untrue, that the name of one of Chaucer's ancestors is found on the roll of Battle Abbey, and that he was born at Woodstock and educated at Merton College, while a foolish way of reading his poems caused him to be connected with "Soler Hall" at Cambridge. Again, the inclusion in an early edition of his works of a poem dated 1402 at one time persuaded antiquaries to postpone his

death till after that year, though the poem is avowedly
by Hoccleve. On the other hand, until quite recent times,
all his biographers assigned his birth to the year 1328,
when, as we now know, his father was still unmarried.
Confusion with Thomas Chaucer caused the poet's name
to be traditionally connected with Woodstock (where,
it is true, he may have resided when in attendance on the
King) and with Donnington, in Berkshire, in both of
which places Thomas Chaucer held property. All these
statements are false, or at least unfounded, but they did
the poet no harm. This, however, was not the case with
the remarkable tissue of assertions which had been woven
out of some passages in the *Testament of Love*, a prose
treatise which cannot possibly be by the poet, who is
expressly mentioned in it as the writer's "master". By
the stupidly imaginative persons to whom this legend was
due Chaucer was represented as having engaged in 1384
in a plot against his patron, Richard II., in consequence
of which he was obliged to flee from justice, remaining
for two years in exile in Hainault, France, and Zealand.
On his venturing to return he was thrown, so we are in-
formed, into prison, and only won his release by dis-
honourably betraying his associates. Fortunately for the
poet's reputation this disgraceful story was demonstrably
false, for during the years of his supposed exile we know
from the State Records that he was living in London and
receiving his pension with his own hands. We now know,
thanks to Professor Skeat and Dr. Henry Bradley, that
running through the first words of the chapters of the
Testament of Love is the acrostic "Margarete of Virtu
have mercy on thin[e] Usk", and its true author is thus
revealed as Thomas Usk, one of the conspirators, who was
executed in March 1388.

CHAPTER II

§ 23. **Chaucer's Reading.**—We have seen something of Chaucer's love of books (§ 20), and now, before we turn to his own career as a poet, we must look at him for a few minutes as a student of the works of other men. The industry of the literary detectives of many nations enables us to track out, probably with no very great incompleteness, the books he had glanced at, the books he had read and used, and the little handful which he seems to have known almost by heart. We have already quoted:

> And as for me, though that I konne but lyte,
> On bokês for to rede I me delyte,
> And to hem give I feyth and ful credence,
> And in myn herte have hem in reverence
> So hertêly, that ther is gamê noon
> That fro my bokês maketh me to goon.

If we thus follow Chaucer into his study we shall be the better able to appreciate both his own poetical development and his unique position in English literature. In a subsequent chapter we shall have to record the various originals from which he translated or otherwise built up many of his poems. Here we have to take a wider glance and consider briefly the works in prose and verse by which he was influenced.

§ 24. **Earlier English Literature.**—Chaucer has often been called the Father of English Poetry, and the phrase is to this extent true that he is the first English poet who exercised an abiding influence on his successors, himself owing practically nothing to earlier English literature. Of the story of Beowulf, of the poems of Caedmon and Cynewulf it is unlikely that he had ever heard, nor is it any more probable that he had ever read a line of Laya-

mon's *Brut* or the *Ormulum*, or that, if either of these
poems had been put into his hands, he could have done
anything more than spell it out with some difficulty. The
French-speaking barons who led the English people in
their struggles for liberty under John and Henry III. did
away with the old hatred of the usurping speech, and for
sixty years the French language gained an ever wider
popularity in England. The danger to the national language was, perhaps, not so great as has sometimes been
represented. While the knowledge of French was spreading among the middle, and even the lower classes, the
use of English was spreading no less among the nobility,
and was soon to gain complete ascendency. But the
nobles could not as yet appreciate literature in the vulgar
tongue, and to English literature the first effect of the
new welding together of classes was disastrous. No important work of English prose and, with the exception
of the *Owl and the Nightingale*, no original English poem
of any length survives from between 1220 and 1300.
During the second and third quarters of this thirteenth
century what Englishmen, even the most patriotic
Englishmen, had to write they wrote either in Latin or
in French, and when, about 1280, composition in English
revived, almost exclusively it took the form of translation. For Chaucer it was with these translations that
English literature began. How far he was acquainted with
the *Cursor Mundi*, the *Ayenbite of Inwyt*, the *Handlyng
Synne*, and the many versions then made of the French
Romances and Lives of the Saints we cannot say. As we
have seen, his family was connected with the Court,
where French was still fashionable, and he himself went
to school before the fashion of construing Latin into
French and not into English had been abandoned. Thus
he probably grew up, as a clever child in Wales may grow
up now, knowing two languages, one as well as the other,

and he may well have preferred in any given case to read a book in the original rather than in an English version. In his delightful parody of the long-winded romances he alluded by name to some seven of them, of most of which English versions still exist, and it is probable that he had glanced at these, if only for the purpose of his parody. But he certainly owed nothing to his predecessors, except that they had set a fashion of translating and imitating from the French, and that it was in this fashion of translation and imitation that he made his first essays in poetry.

§ 25. **Mediaeval Latin Literature.**—The place of the older vernacular literature was supplied for Chaucer by the Latin poetry and prose in which, for a few centuries, the literary ability of all Europe found a common meeting ground. The writers of the twelfth century were his chief favourites, and in the twelfth century the English Latinists were at their best. There are references or quotations in Chaucer which show that he knew at least four of the chief of these—Geoffrey of Monmouth, "English Galfrid", as he calls him, whose *Historia Britonum* shocked serious historians by its tales of the Trojans in Britain and the Court of Arthur; Walter Map, whose anti-matrimonial treatise, *Valerius ad Rufinum de non ducenda uxore*, supplied the poet with some of his too many gibes at women; Nigel Wireker, whose *Speculum Stultorum*, or tale of "Dan Burnell the Ass", hit so hard at the follies and vices of the time; and John of Salisbury, the secretary of Thomas à Becket, and the author of the *Polycraticus sive De Nugis Curialium*, which embraced at once a satire on the vices of courts and a bold contribution to the controversy between church and king. Among the Latin works of this twelfth century written by foreigners Chaucer also knew well the prose treatise *De Contemptu Mundi sive de Miseria Conditionis Humanae* of the great mediaeval pope, Innocent III., and, moreover, trans-

lated it, either in whole or part. He knew, too, the works
of Alain de l'Isle (Alanus de Insulis), the Cistercian Bishop
of Auxerre, three of which he quotes or refers to; also the
Alexandreis of Gualtier de Lille. From his readings in the
authors of the thirteenth century we may note his reference to Bradwardine's treatise, *De Causa Dei*, his use of
the great collection of lives of the saints, the *Golden
Legend* of Jacobus de Voragine, Archbishop of Genoa,
and of the *Historia Trojana*, in which Guido delle
Colonne, borrowing from his forgotten predecessor,
Benoît de Sainte Maur, summed up the mediaeval legends
of the story of Troy. To complete this list, as far as it has
yet been made out, the names of about a dozen more
Latinists might be added, but with these we need not
concern ourselves. What we have here to note is the
abundance of the Latin literature of the twelfth and
thirteenth centuries, and the fact that Chaucer was well
acquainted with it.

§ 26. **Classical Literature.**—This is, perhaps, the best
place to glance for a moment at the extent of Chaucer's
acquaintance with the masterpieces of classical Latin.
Here his reading appears to have been that of the ordin-
ary literary man of his day. To him, as to others, these
storehouses of tales, the *Metamorphoses* and *Heroides* of
Ovid, were thoroughly familiar, and he knew also some
of his other works. Virgil's *Aeneid* also he knew well, and
the *Thebaid* of Statius, with some of the works of Claud-
ian, and a little of Juvenal and Persius. Though he frequently alludes to Livy it is doubtful if he knew either
this author or Suetonius at first hand, or anything of
Cicero save his *De Divinatione* and the incident of Scipio's
Dream (*Somnium Scipionis*) in the *Republic*. On the
other hand, with Seneca and Boethius (whose *De Consolatione Philosophiae* he translated) he was probably
far better acquainted than any poet of the present day.

In common with his contemporaries, Chaucer was also well read in two Latin works of the fifth century—the Commentary of the Neo-Platonist Macrobius on the *Somnium Scipionis* mentioned above, and Marcian's *De Nuptiis Philologiae et Mercurii*, a scientific treatise enlivened by a pretty romance of the marriage of Learning and Mercury. Of Greek, it is needless to say, he knew nothing, his knowledge of the Tale of Troy being derived from Virgil and Guido and the Latin translations from the Greek forgeries assigned to Dares Phrygius and Dictys Cretensis. Of the Latin version of the Bible his knowledge, if not very accurate, was considerable.

§ 27. **French Literature.**—As we have seen, the translation and imitation of French poems and treatises formed the first-fruits of the revival of English literature which took place in the half-century preceding Chaucer's birth, and he himself followed this fashion. The great poem which he selected to translate was the *Roman de la Rose*, and later on we shall have to consider whether the extant translation of portions of this work is wholly or in any part by Chaucer. But quite apart from this thorny question a knowledge of the nature and contents of the French poem is essential to a right understanding of Chaucer's development, for it exercised on him an influence greater than that of any other single work, supplying him with poetic forms and machinery which he was slow to outgrow, and with reminiscences of particular passages which leave their trace on some of his best and latest work. We must, therefore, find space for a brief account of this remarkable poem.

§ 28. **Guillaume de Lorris.**—The *Roman de la Rose* consists in all of rather over 22,000 octosyllabic lines rhyming in couplets. The first part of the poem—some 4150 in length—was written about 1237 by a young clerk named Guillaume de Lorris, who died before he could bring it to a completion. In his poem he feigns that in his twentieth year he had fallen asleep, and dreamed that on a beautiful morning in May he had come to a garden surrounded by a high wall, on the outer side of which were painted all the disagreeable vices and troubles of life—Hatred, Covetousness, Sadness, Old Age, Hypocrisy, Poverty, and the like—as if to show that within the garden these could have no place. Attracted by the song of the birds he searched for an entrance, and at length found a little gate guarded by a fair maiden named Idleness, who told him that the garden belonged to Sir Mirth, and allowed him to enter. Soon he espies Mirth accompanied by Dame Gladness and the God of Love himself, attended by a bachelor, Sweet-Looking, who carried bows and arrows. With them were many fair ladies—Beauty, Riches, Largesse, Fraunchise, and Courtesy—all of whom are elaborately described. Then he surveys all the garden, and comes to the well where Narcissus perished, and at last approaches a rose-bush, and essays to pull one of the buds. As he hesitates, Love pierces him with his arrows, and henceforth all his thoughts are set on obtaining the rosebud. He becomes Love's vassal, and receives his commandments, rather tediously conveyed in some 800 lines. "Bel Accueil" (Good Reception) then helps him, but he is hindered by "Danger" (Guardianship), Slander, Shame, and Fear. He attempts too hastily to kiss the Rose, and is repulsed, and Reason then essays to argue him out of his passion. Fraunchise (Generosity), Pity, and Venus herself befriend him, but Slander and Jealousy are now aroused, and Bel Accueil, without whose help he cannot obtain the Rose, is imprisoned in a tower. The Lover then begins a lament, and in the midst of this monologue the poem breaks off abruptly. If, like many other mediaeval compositions, a little tedious, so far as Guillaume de Lorris carried it, this wooing of the Rose is a very charming

poem, full of skilful descriptions and instinct with the
sentiment of the time. The dream, the May morning, the
fair garden, the allegory, and personifications, all these
became part of the machinery of later poets, and, as we
shall see, Chaucer did not fail to avail himself of them,
like the rest.

§ 29. **Jean de Meung.**—More than forty years after the
death of Guillaume de Lorris his unfinished work was
taken up by another young poet, Jean Clopinel, called
from his birthplace Jean de Meung, then a student at
Paris. The metre of the continuation was the same as that
of the original, many of the characters were the same, the
interrupted lamentation of the Lover was duly taken up
and finished, and his suit of the Rose brought to a happy
end; but the spirit of the poem was wholly changed.
Guillaume de Lorris had set out to write an allegory of
Love as the fair ladies of his day imagined it; his continuator wrote on every topic of mediaeval life, and his
standpoint was not that of the fair ladies but that of their
bitter satirist. When the Lover ceases lamenting, Reason
argues with him once more, this time in a speech of 3000
lines, after which, at scarcely less length, "Ami", the
Friend, details to him all the tricks of mediaeval intrigue.
False-Seeming, who is wont to attire himself as a Dominican friar, entraps and murders Slander, one of the four
guardians of the castle, and the Duenna, "la Vieille", a
very hateful person, is gained over to the Lover's side.
But still the Rose cannot be won. A set battle ensues, in
which the allegorical personages show their prowess, but
though helped by Venus herself, the Lover is again repulsed. Art and Nature are called to aid, and at the bidding of Nature Genius disarms all opposition; so at last
the beautiful Rose is won, and the sleeper awakes. But
in the second part the story has become a mere thread
on which to string endless discourses, in which questions

of life and conduct, of destiny and free will, of religion and morals, of marriage and celibacy, are unsparingly handled. Against women and against the clergy, especially the Dominicans, the satire is merciless and unceasing, and the poem was severely condemned, not to the diminution of its popularity. To Chaucer it was a storehouse from which he was never tired of drawing, and his own intellectual life may be represented, not unjustly, as a progress from the standpoint of Guillaume de Lorris to that of Jean de Meung. For the latter, bold as he was, was not irreligious, and some of his other works, which also Chaucer had read, are said to exhibit a most sincere piety. Like many another good Catholic, he satirised the accidental weaknesses of a religion in which he none the less believed, and we shall find later on that in this also Chaucer imitated him.

§ 30. **Other French Writers.**—In addition to the two parts of the *Roman de la Rose* and some of the other works of Jean de Meung, Chaucer was acquainted with and used the Anglo-Norman chronicle of Nicolas Trivet and the *Pèlerinaige de la vie humaine* (prototype of our *Pilgrim's Progress*) of Guillaume de Deguilleville, both writers of the first half of the fourteenth century. Next, however, to Jean de Meung, the French writer who influenced him most was Guillaume de Machault. From Machault he may, perhaps, have made a translation, the *Book of the Lion*, which is mentioned among his works, but has long been lost. Imitations of Machault have also been traced in some of Chaucer's extant poems, and it was from Machault that the English poet borrowed his two most successful metres, the seven-line stanza and the decasyllabic couplet. With Machault's disciple, Eustache Deschamps, who hailed him as "grand translateur, noble Geoffroy Chaucer", our poet was on terms of literary friendship; as also with the chronicler Froissart and Sir

Otes de Granson, a pensioner of Richard II., and "flour of hem that make in Fraunce", from whom he translated a group of short poems. At a time when Englishmen were still writing verse in French the intercourse between the poets of the two nations must have been considerable, despite the constant wars, and Chaucer himself was doubtless familiar with much contemporary French verse which has left no mark on his own poetry. But the intellectual influence of the *Roman de la Rose* and the metrical influence of Guillaume de Machault stand out as two important factors contributed by French literature to our poet's development.

§ 31. **Italian Literature—Dante.**—As we have seen (§ 12), Chaucer's first mission to Italy lasted from 1st December 1372 to 23rd May of the following year. A half-century had only just elapsed since the death of the great national poet (14th September 1321), broken-hearted and in exile, but already Florence was establishing a Dante professorship, and on 23rd October 1373, only a few months after Chaucer had left Italy, the first lecture was delivered by no less a man than Boccaccio. To a fame thus established the English poet was not likely to be indifferent, and an invocation to the Blessed Virgin, imitated from the *Paradiso*, canto xxxiii., occurs in a poem which may have been written before his second visit to Italy, though it bears some appearance of being a later addition. After Chaucer's return from his second mission in 1379 references to Dante are more frequent, and show a wider acquaintance with his great work, so that we may guess that the poet was then able to purchase a complete manuscript of the *Divina Commedia* for himself. Of Dante's other works he appears to have been ignorant, and even the *Divine Comedy* does not seem to have directly influenced more than a hundred lines of his poetry. But two interesting fragments have justly been ascribed to him in which he uses Dante's metre; and it has been maintained that in one of his poems, the *Hous of Fame*, he takes the form of the *Commedia* as his model. The temper of the two poets was widely different, and Chaucer, of whom a contemporary, doubtless ignorant of Italian, could say that he had written "Dante in English", though indebted to his great predecessor artistically, imbibed none of his sternness of soul.

§ 32. **Boccaccio.**—Far more important than that of Dante was the influence upon Chaucer of his own contemporary, Boccaccio, and, if we may believe him, of "Fraunceys Petrark, the laureat poete", whom he even speaks of in one place as "my master". Yet of Petrarch Chaucer's works only prove an acquaintance with his Latin version of Boccaccio's tale of Grisilde, and with a single sonnet (the eighty-eighth). To Boccaccio's *Teseide* and *Filostrato*, on the other hand, he was indebted for something more than the groundwork of two of his most important poems; and he was also acquainted with three of his works in Latin prose. If, as is somewhat hardily maintained, he also knew the *Decamerone* and took from it, in however improved a fashion, the idea of his Canterbury Pilgrimage and the plots of any or all of the four tales (besides that of Grisilde) to which resemblances have been traced in his own work, his obligations to Boccaccio become immense. Yet he never mentions his name, and it has been contended that he was himself unaware of the authorship of the poems and treatises to which he was so greatly indebted. Strange as this seems to us, it is by no means incredible; for it was the exception rather than the rule for a fourteenth-century manuscript to mention the name of its author, unless posthumous fame had made it important; and there is some good ground for believing that Chaucer imagined himself indebted to Petrarch for the works which were really

Boccaccio's. Whether this be so or not, and whether Boccaccio be hidden behind that mysterious "auctor Lollius", to whom Chaucer alludes as an authority on the history of Troy, we need not here inquire.

§ 33. **Variety of Chaucer's Reading.**—Just as all we know about Chaucer's career in the King's service has been laboriously pieced together out of dull records of old payments, so the foregoing account of the chief literary influences which swayed his career as a poet is based upon the industry of the scholars who have tracked to their sources the references, quotations, and parallels which they found in his works, and have thus enabled us to identify the books which he had read, so we may fairly conclude, with the greatest interest. Both in the one field and in the other fresh discoveries may yet be made, but we have good reason to be grateful for what has already been done. The prosaic realities of Chaucer's life are ten times more varied and interesting than the career which Leland provided for him; and if he was by no means so "acute" a "logician", so "profound" a "philosopher", or so "able" a "mathematician" as Leland would have us believe, abundant proof has been obtained of both the width and the wisdom of his reading. When we remember the costliness of books in the fourteenth century, we may well rejoice that Chaucer was lucky enough to obtain so many that were really useful to the development of his genius.

CHAPTER III

THE CONTENTS AND ORDER OF CHAUCER'S WRITINGS

§ 34. **Early Printed Editions of Chaucer.**—In the days when all books were in manuscript it was only very rarely indeed that the writings of an author were collected into a single volume, or set of volumes, and labelled his "Works". No such manuscript of Chaucer is known to exist, and when William Caxton, with wise promptitude, probably the year after he set up his press at Westminster, began to print Chaucer's writings, he issued those he was able to obtain in at least six different volumes. To his edition of the *Book of Fame* Caxton added a commendation of the poem and its author, which shows the estimation in which Chaucer was held towards the close of the first century after his death. "For he toucheth in it", Caxton says, "right great wisdom and subtle understanding, and so in all his works he excelleth in mine opinion all other writers in our English. For he writeth no void words, but all his matter is full of high and quick sentence: to whom ought to be given laud and praising for his noble making and writing. For of him all others have borrowed since and taken, in all their well saying and doing." So thought Caxton, and doubtless if he had been able to obtain a complete set of manuscripts, he would gladly have printed everything that Chaucer ever wrote. But collected editions were not yet the fashion, and it was not until 1532, after the lapse of another half-century, that a single volume professing to contain all of Chaucer's works was at last issued, under the editorship of William Thynne.

In 1532 Chaucer had been dead 132 years, and his fame was very great. Everybody knew that he was the author of the *Canterbury Tales* and *Troilus and Criseyde*, but the difficulty of determining his minor works was doubtless considerable. Thynne took the right course, and erred on the side of liberality, preserving several poems, some good, some poor, which we now know could not have been written by Chaucer. The poet's fame acted as a magnet, and subsequent editors imitated Thynne's liberality only too freely. Many poems, some of them very unworthy of him, have thus been wrongly attributed to Chaucer, and it is only within the last century that these have been successfully separated from his real work. This has been done by placing on one side the poems of his authorship of which we have absolute and indisputable evidence, and examining their language and system of versification. The result of this examination is to show that, both as regards language and versification, Chaucer's usages were quite remarkably consistent, and that they differed in many important respects from those of other poets of his time. A brief account of these usages will be found in a subsequent chapter. For the present we may be content in the first place to ascertain what poems can be proved by certain evidence to be Chaucer's, and to confine ourselves at first to these. The knowledge we shall thus gain will help us hereafter in deciding on the claims of the other pieces which have been attributed to him to be really his.

§ 35. **Works ascribed to Chaucer by himself and his Contemporaries.**—We might fairly take the authenticity of the poems assigned to Chaucer by Caxton in the century after his death as a matter of notoriety, but we need not do so. His younger contemporary Lydgate (1370?–1445?) mentions Chaucer as the author of the *Canterbury Tales*, and in the conversation which takes place before one of these tales (that assigned to the Man of Law) Chaucer refers at some length to his *Legende of Good Women*, which he calls, quaintly enough, "the seintes legendes of Cupide", *i.e.* the Legends of Cupid's Saints. Now in a remarkable passage in the *Legende* he gives a list of his principal works up to the date of writing, and names specifically a translation of the *Roman de la Rose, Troilus and Criseyde*, the *Hous of Fame*, the *Dethe of Blaunche the Duchesse*, the *Parlement of Foules*, and his prose translation of Boethius's *De Consolatione*. All his

chief works are thus inseparably linked together, and we
may join to them the *Lines to Adam Scrivener*, in which
the author of *Troilus* and the *Boece* complains of the carelessness with which they have been copied out. But again,
Lydgate, in the same prologue to his *Fall of Princes*, in
which he mentions the *Canterbury Tales*, also mentions
as Chaucer's (besides most of the works already enumerated) the story of *Anelida and Arcyte* and (by allusion
to one passage in it) the *Compleynt of Mars*, as also the
prose treatise on the Astrolabe, which Chaucer addressed
to his little son Lewis. The same contemporary, in his
translation of Guillaume de Deguilleville's *Pèlerinaige de
la vie humaine*, further alludes to a translation by Chaucer
of a hymn to the Blessed Virgin, which occurs in it, and
is known as the *A B C*. Seven other poems are vouched
for as Chaucer's by John Shirley (1366?–1456), an earnest
lover of the poet, and, like Lydgate, born sufficiently
early, if dates can be trusted, to have known him personally. These seven poems are the *Exclamacion of the Dethe
of Pite* (usually quoted as the *Compleynt to Pite*, from the
title of its second part), *Fortune, Truth, Gentilesse, Lak
of Stedfastnesse*, a triplet of ballades translated from Sir
Otes de Granson, miscalled by Shirley the *Compleynt of
Venus*, and the *Compleynt to his Empty Purs*. To these
we may add an eighth, the set of metrical experiments
called by Professor Skeat Chaucer's *Compleynt to his
Lady*. These, though not specifically headed as Chaucer's,
are joined on by Shirley to his copy of the *Pite*, and thus
sufficiently avouched. Lastly, we have the evidence of
reasonably good manuscripts for the ascription to Chaucer
of the newly discovered *To Rosemounde*, of the *Envoy
to Scogan*, the *Envoy to Bukton*, the *Former Age*, and
the two quatrains known as Chaucer's *Proverbs*, and
with these we close the list of the poems for whose
authenticity we can produce external evidence. For

greater clearness we may look at them again, arranged in a table:

Common notoriety confirmed by Lyd-gate.	avouches	*Canterbury Tales.*
Canterbury Tales (Man of Law's Head-link) . .	,,	*Legende of Good Women.*
Legende of Good Wo-men	,,	A translation of the *Roman de la Rose.* *Troilus and Criseyde.* *Hous of Fame.* *Dethe of Blaunche.* *Parlement of Foules.* *Boece* (prose). (*Lines to Adam Scrivener.*)
Lydgate— i. In Prologue to *Fall of Princes*	,,	**Anelida and Arcyte.* **Compleynt of Mars.* *Astrolabe* (prose).
ii. In Translation of Deguilleville	,,	**A B C.* * *Ascribed to Chaucer also by Shirley.*
Shirley MSS. . . .	,,	*Pite.* *Compleynt to his Lady* (copied as a continuation of *Pite*). *Fortune.* *Truth.* *Gentilesse.* *Lak of Stedfastnesse.* Ballades from Granson (called *Compleynt of Venus*). *Compleynt to his Purs.*
Ascription in other Manuscripts	,,	*To Rosemounde.* *Envoy to Scogan.* *Envoy to Bukton.* *The Former Age.* *Proverbs.*

§ 36. **Corroborative Evidence of Genuineness.**—The foregoing table exhibits fairly well the comparative weight of external evidence in favour of the ascription to Chaucer of each of the poems it contains. For the more important poems we are fortunate in having the testimony of Chaucer himself, although in the one case of the translation of the *Roman de la Rose* it is disputed whether the testimony refers to the version which has actually come down to us or to another translation now lost. For three out of twelve other pieces we have the witness both of Lydgate and Shirley, for one of Lydgate alone, and for eight only of Shirley. Four other poems are avouched by anonymous scribes, whose ascriptions do not carry the weight of Shirley or Lydgate. Here, however, internal evidence comes to help us out. In the first place, the usages as to metre and language which we find observed in the poems claimed by Chaucer himself (putting on one side the *Romaunt of the Rose*) are observed also in all the other poems on our list, and as Chaucer's usages were much stricter than those of his contemporaries, save perhaps Gower, this negative evidence is a strong corroboration of a scribe's assertion. In the second place, some special argument of authenticity can be brought forward in favour of almost every several poem, and in some instances these arguments are so strong that Chaucer's authorship is as certain as in the case of the *Canterbury Tales* themselves. Thus—to take the last four poems on our list—in the *Envoy to Bukton* there is an allusion to the Wife of Bath, a lady very prominent in the *Tales*; in the *Envoy to Scogan* there are allusions which exactly fit in with what we know from other sources of Chaucer's circumstances and employments (§ 18); *The Former Age* is practically a translation of one of the "metres" or interludes in verse in Boethius's *De Consolatione* (translated by Chaucer into prose), and has a family connection with the four poems *Fortune, Truth, sqq.* on the Shirley list. Even the two rather insignificant *Proverbs* can claim that the adage on which one of them is founded is, as Professor Skeat has remarked, quoted in one of the *Canterbury*

Tales. If anyone pleases to maintain that they are not Chaucer's, the *Proverbs* are not worth fighting for, though as attributed to him on fair authority they may be allowed a place among his works. Of the other poems on the list (always excepting the *Romaunt*) the authenticity is indisputable.

§ 37. **Three Points raised by List in "Legende of Good Women".**—We must now return once more to the list which Chaucer gives of his own writings in his Prologue to the *Legende of Good Women.* As a pleasant change from our table we may quote the passage somewhat fully. The poet tells us how, after gazing on his favourite flower, the daisy, he had gone to sleep in a little "herber" or arbour, and dreamed that he saw the God of Love approaching him with his Queen and nineteen fair ladies. The God of Love asked who he was, and on learning, upbraided him as one unworthy to approach the daisy:

> Quod he "what dostow heer,
> So nigh myn owné flour, so boldély?
> For it were better worthy, trewély,
> A worm to neghen neer my flour than thou."
> "And why, sir," quod I, "and hit lyké yow?"
> "For thou," quod he, "art therto nothing able;
> Hit is my relik, digne and delytáble,
> And thou my fo, and al my folk werreyest,
> And of myn oldé servaunts thou misseyest,
> And hindrest hem, with thy translacioun,
> And lettest folk from hir devocioun
> To servé me, and holdest hit folye
> To servé Love. Thou mayst hit nat denye;
> For in pleyn texte, withouten nede of glose,
> Thou hast translated the *Romaunce of the Rose,*
> That is an heresye ageyns my lawe,
> And makest wysé folk fro me withdrawe,
> And of *Creseyde* thou hast said as thee liste,
> That maketh men to wommen lassé triste,
> That ben as trewe as ever was any steel."

But the Queen of Love pleads in Chaucer's behalf, and puts forward his writings on the other side.

All be hit that he can nat wel endyte,

she says compassionately,

> Yet hath he makèd lewèd folk delyte
> To servè you, in preysing of your name.
> He made the book that hight the *Hous of Fame,*
> And eek the *Deeth of Blaunche the Duchesse,*
> And the *Parlement of Foulès,* as I gesse,
> And al the love of *Palamon and Arcyte*
> Of Thebès, thogh the story is knowen lyte ;
> And many an ympnè for your halydayes,
> That highten *Balades, Roundels, Virelayes;*
> And, for to speke of other holynesse,
> He hath in prosè translated *Boëce*
> [And of the *Wrecched Engendring of Mankynde,*
> As men may in Pope Innocent y-fynde;]
> And mad the *Lyf* also of *Seynt Cecyle;*
> He made also, goon sithen a greet whyle,
> *Origenes upon the Maudeleyne;*
> Him oghtè now to have the lessè peyne;
> He hath mad many a lay and many a thing.

Now in addition to the information it has already yielded us, this passage makes clear three very important points:

(i.) That several of Chaucer's poems are now lost.

(ii) That he was in the habit of recasting his work.

(iii.) That when he began to write his *Canterbury Tales* he included among them some poems which he already had by him.

On each of these points we must say a few words.

(i.) Lost Works and their Fate.—It will be noted that in the passage quoted mention is made not only of many *Balades, Roundels, Virelayes,* which are hardly at all represented in Chaucer's works, as we now have them, but also of two longer ones which have disappeared, translations of Innocent III.'s treatise, *De Miseria Conditionis Humanae* (§ 25), and of the homily on St. Mary Magdalene, falsely attributed to Origen. By Lydgate, again, and in a list of Chaucer's works given in most manuscripts at the end of the *Canterbury Tales* (see § 77),

there is mention of a *Book of the Lion,* supposed to have
been a translation of *Le Dit du Lion* by Guillaume
Machault (§ 30). Perhaps we should add that in the Man
of Law's Head-link in the *Tales* it is said of Chaucer:

> In youthe he made of Ceys and Alcioun;

and by Lydgate also there is a reference to

> The pytous story of Ceix and Alcion
> And the Deth also of Blaunche the Duchesse.

But as the incident of Ceyx and Alcione occupies no less
than 158 out of the 290 lines which form the proem to the
Dethe, we may fairly assume that it is important enough
to be named separately without insisting on the possibility of its having formed the chief subject of an independent poem now lost. None of the other works now
exist, but at least one of them seems to have left traces
in a poem which has come down to us. Prefixed to the
Man of Law's Tale is a prologue on the evils of poverty,
which has little or no connection with the story. Four out
of the five stanzas of this prologue are translated from
Innocent III., as are also three several other stanzas and
one half-stanza in the body of the tale. It seems at least
possible that Chaucer was here using up old work. There
is also the case of *Palamon and Arcyte,* as to which some
good scholars have believed that, previously to the version in the Knight's Tale, Chaucer had composed a more
literal translation of Boccaccio's *Teseide* in seven-line
stanzas, and that this earlier poem he withdrew from
circulation, using fragments of it as the basis for ten
stanzas in *Anelida and Arcyte,* for three in *Troilus and
Criseyde,* and for sixteen in the *Parlement of Foules.* It is
more likely, however, that these stanzas were reminiscences of the original and that the poem survives in the
Knight's Tale.

(ii.) CHAUCER'S REVISION OF HIS WORK.—It may have

been noted that two of the lines quoted on page 41 are in brackets. This is because they are taken from a version of the Prologue differing from the rest. Both versions exist in their entirety, and the differences between them are considerable; so here is another instance in which Chaucer rewrote his own work. These extreme examples will prepare us to find that in other poems also Chaucer made alterations and additions at a date subsequent to that of their first composition.

(iii.) EARLY POEMS AMONG THE "CANTERBURY TALES". —In the quotation from the *Legende* there is a reference to a *Lyf of Seint Cecyle*, but we find this Lyf among the *Canterbury Tales*, where it is assigned to the Second Nun. In its place there it still retains marks that it was not originally composed as one of the *Tales*, for in the preliminary Invocation to the Blessed Virgin the narrator is spoken of as a "*son* of Eve", and asks the forgiveness of "yow that reden that I wryte". We cannot imagine that Chaucer would have deliberately made a nun, telling a story to riders along the highroad, speak of herself as a man, and of her audience as her readers, and we are forced to believe that the poem was originally written with no reference to the Canterbury Pilgrimage. If this be so with one tale it may be so with others, and we shall not be surprised, therefore, if we find that there are four poems, perhaps five or even more, which were probably written before the scheme of the Canterbury Pilgrimage assumed shape, and afterwards inserted into it with such amount of revision as Chaucer could find time for.

§ 38. **Order and Dates of Chaucer's Works.**—A complete chronology of Chaucer's writings is difficult because (i) if we count each Canterbury Tale separately he produced no fewer than forty-five pieces in verse and four in prose; (ii) there is a high probability that he was sometimes working on two or more of these at the same time;

and (iii) in the case of several of the Canterbury Tales the evidence is mainly derived from style and temper and we cannot be sure how far we are justified in bringing poems in which these are similar close together in order of time, or again how far the comparative failure of the Doctor's Tale of Appius and Virginia and the Manciple's of Phoebus and the Crow may be taken as a proof of early work. Nevertheless, to supply the lack of dated first editions such as we look for from poets who have written since printing was invented, we have considerable help in determining the sequence in which the bulk of Chaucer's works were written and some guidance to the years during which he was working on them.

(1) ALLUSIONS FROM POEM TO POEM.—Our first great help in determining the order of Chaucer's writings is that we know that the *Canterbury Tales* in their collected form are later than the *Legende of Good Women*, to which allusion is made in the Man of Law's Head-link (§ 35), and that the *Legende* also is necessarily later than any of the seven extant and two lost works which are enumerated in its prologue. On the other hand, Chaucer's words towards the end of his *Troilus* (v. 1786–88):

> Go, litel book! Go, litel myn tragédie!
> Ther God thy maker yit, or that he dye,
> So sendè might to make in som comédie!

have been much less helpful, since three different identifications of this projected comedy have been suggested. The first, strongly supported by Skeat, finds it in the *Hous of Fame*, regarded as a far-off imitation of the *Divina Commedia* of Dante, from which details of various kinds are borrowed; the second, which Professor Kittredge seems to favour, finds not in the *Hous of Fame* but in the *Canterbury Tales*, considered as a whole, a human comedy not unworthy to be set beside Dante's divine one; a third, propounded by the present writer in his edition of the Knight's Tale in 1903, makes the humble point that as the story of *Palamon and Arcyte* begins with Palamon wounded and in prison and ends with his happy marriage it is the antithesis of a tragedy as defined by Chaucer—"the harm of hem that stood in high degree" (Monk's Tale, B. 3182)—and so may well be the comedy which he projected as a counterpoise to his *Troilus*.

(2) EXTERNAL REFERENCES.—Turning now to these we find that the death of the Duchess Blanche, 12th September 1369, dates the poem in her honour 1369–70. The marriage of Richard II. with Anne of Bohemia, 14th January 1382, after negotiations begun on 12th December 1380, helps to date four poems: (i) *The Hous of Fame* as starting from a dream on 10th December, presumed to be that night in 1380 when the decision to send an embassy was probably first known; (ii) *The Parlement of Foules* as an allegory of the courting of Anne by three suitors; (iii) *Troilus* in virtue of l. 172, "Right as our firste lettre is now an A"; (iv) *The Legende of Good Women*, in which (in the earlier form of the Prologue) the poem was to be given her "at Eltham or at Shene". Allusions to events connected with the marriage have also been seen in Knight's Tale, l. 26, "and of the tempest at her hoom-comynge" and in the mention in l. 2112 *sq.* of "a parlement" at Athens "to have with certein contrees alliaunce", these being construed as referring to a storm or tidal wave when Anne crossed the Channel and to an English parliament about alliance with Bohemia in November 1381. The poems called the *Compleynt of Venus* are translated from Sir Otes de Granson, a Savoyard, who was in England from 1391 to 1396, and at the close of 1393 received a pension from Richard II. Chaucer is said to have made his translation at the request of Isabella of York, who died in 1394, and we may therefore reasonably place it about the year 1393, when Granson was in favour at Court. In the *Envoy*

to Scogan there appears to be an allusion to the heavy rains of the autumn of 1393, and this seems confirmed by Chaucer dating the poem from Greenwich, where his work as Commissioner of the Roadway between Woolwich and Greenwich would take him about that time (§ 18). In the *Envoy to Bukton* Professor Skeat has drawn attention to the allusion to the English expedition to Friesland, which lasted from August to October 1396. Lastly the poem entitled the *Compleynt to his Purs* must be connected with the grant by Henry IV. of the pension of 40 marks in October 1399 (§ 19). In this way we obtain certain dates for some poems and approximate ones for others.

(3) REFERENCES TO THE CALENDAR, TO ASTRONOMY AND ASTROLOGY.—Although in his work on the Astrolabe Chaucer disclaimed belief in the influence of the planets on human lives, in the construction of his plots he availed himself of this belief quite frequently. Owing to the Greek and Arabic sources from which nearly all the mediaeval knowledge of medicine was derived, the belief, as is shown in Chaucer's sketch of the "Doctor of Phisik", played a great part in medical practice, and probably spread thence to other departments of the business of life. By a process at once arbitrary and unchristian the planets were associated with Greek gods and goddesses and their dominant qualities in Greek mythology; also each day of the week and each hour of the day was thought to be influenced for good or evil respectively by Saturn, Jupiter, Mars, the Sun (Apollo), Venus, Mercury, and the Moon (Diana). Thus men who believed, or played with, astrology thought it necessary to choose lucky days and hours for beginning any enterprise and to avoid unlucky ones. At the back of this lay a much more complicated system based on the positions of the planets in the twelve signs of the Zodiac, named after the groups of fixed stars

which cluster round successive sections of their path: Aries the ram, Taurus the bull, Gemini the twins, etc. To this Chaucer often alludes (*e.g.* Prologue, 414-18; Man of Law's Tale, 295-315), but as knowledge of it required considerable study he does not often enter into details. Everyone, however, knew about the days of the week, more especially that Friday, dominated by the caprices of Venus, was unlucky, also that two or more days in every month were traditionally very unlucky, and others only a little less so.   Chaucer makes use of this latter belief as regards the dates 3rd May, 6th May, and (probably) 8th June. The first of these, 3rd May, he uses no less than three times to mark the unlucky beginning of an adventure, and in the case of the Knight's Tale, to make the day which Palamon chose to break out of prison even more disastrous, he made that particular 3rd May fall on a Friday, in pursuance of a scheme by which the principal events in the story are assigned to their astrologically appropriate days and hours. Astrological appropriateness being Chaucer's aim, it is evident that the fact that 3rd May fell on a Friday in 1387 gives no ground for the deduction drawn by Dr. Skeat that the Knight's Tale was probably written in that year. In the same way it is regrettable that the *Hous of Fame* has been assigned to 1383, because it starts from a dream on a certain 10th December and contains references to Jupiter, and in 1383 10th December fell on a Thursday, Jupiter's day. The relevance of the date, 10th December, is probably, as suggested by Dr. Brusendorff, that on that day in 1380 the decision was taken to send ambassadors (formally appointed on the 12th) to treat for Richard II.'s marriage with Anne of Bohemia. If so, the inception of the *Hous of Fame* is brought back to 1381. As for the Knight's Tale, freed from the misconception that it must have been written in a year in which days of the months fell on days of the week convenient for the story, it becomes the tale of "al the love of Palamon and Arcite" pleaded in extenuation of Chaucer's misdoings in the prologue to the *Legende of Good Women*, which it must therefore precede.

On the other hand, a simple observation of the heavens introduced incidentally may be really helpful for dating. Thus, as Dr. Koch first noted, in ll. 117-119 of the *Parlement of Foules*, Chaucer tells us that he began to write this poem when the star Venus was visible in the north-west, *i.e.* as an evening star. This can only happen in the months of May, June, July, or August, and not in every year. Astronomers tell us that Venus was thus visible in 1374, 1377, 1380, 1382, and 1383, but not in 1381; and as for other reasons our choice of dates for this poem is confined to 1381 and 1382, we may feel fairly certain that it was written in the summer of 1382.

§ 39. **Internal Evidence of Date.**—(1) ITALIAN INFLUENCE.—As the facts collected in the last few sections have gradually been published they have put rather a new aspect upon a generalisation which has yet done excellent service in settling the chronology of Chaucer's poems. By Ten Brink and the early workers for the Chaucer Society the year of Chaucer's first visit to Italy was taken as a dividing line, and every poem which showed the influence of any Italian poet was on that ground assigned a date subsequent to 1373. As against this principle of arrangement Professor Manly has urged that Chaucer had something of the same inducement to learn foreign languages as a modern young diplomat, and that there were Italians in London from whom he could have learnt their language. The question need not be argued, for the use of the first visit to Italy as a dividing line having served its purpose by offering a provisional grouping of Chaucer's poems, may now be put aside since we know by other evidence

the approximate dates of almost all the poems not included in the *Canterbury Tales*. We know that the *Dethe
of Blaunche*, which shows no trace of Italian influence,
was written in 1369, and the *Hous of Fame, Parlement of
Foules, Troilus and Criseyde*, and *Palamon and Arcyte*,
all of them indebted to Italian models, all fall within the
five or six years between the negotiations for Richard
II.'s marriage and the writing of the Prologue to the
Legende of Good Women. There is no longer any reason
to argue from the inherent improbability of Chaucer's
acquaintance with *Dante* or *Boccaccio* before 1372. There
is positive evidence that the poems which show traces of
this acquaintance are, as the old argument anticipated, of
a later date. Nay, more, it cannot but strike us that every
one of the poems we have named belongs to a date subsequent to 1379, *i.e.* subsequent not only to the first but
also to the second visit to Italy. The question arises, Was
it not after the later of the two Italian missions that
the influence of Italian literature was for the first time
strongly felt? The paraphrase of Dante in the Invocation
to the Blessed Virgin prefixed to the *Lyf of Seint Cecyle*
seems to be the only poem presumably written before
1379 in which there is a trace of Italian influence, and we
need not try to find a later date for this to make a new
dividing line at 1378. Chaucer may have read Dante and
Boccaccio on his first visit to Italy, and even have made
extracts from them, but it does not follow that he bought
manuscripts of their works to take home with him. Up to
the date of this mission he had had no very lucrative
employments—when he went to France in 1369 he had
to borrow £10 from a friend—and though his allowance
on this occasion was considerable, it is doubtful if it left
him any great margin for book-buying, at the price which
books then cost. Moreover, if any books were purchased
on this visit, it is more likely that they were Latin ones

than Italian, written in the language which Chaucer knew well, rather than in that which he was probably only just acquiring, and we know in fact of two Latin books by Boccaccio which it is probable he did obtain on this occasion. This is not the place in which to insist on merely personal opinions, but it seems at least possible that Chaucer's intimate use of Italian literature should be dated from 1379 rather than 1372, and we shall find that this theory is certainly no hindrance, but rather a help, to our understanding Chaucer's development. The only poems which it will help us to date are the *Compleynt to his Lady* and the closely connected *Anelida and Arcyte*, both of which appear to have been written shortly after 1380.

(2) EVIDENCE OF METRE.—We have seen that the knowledge-of-Italian test in its original form comes to be rather a convenient generalisation of what we know by other evidence than a real witness to the date of any given poem, and we shall find that this applies to most of the other internal tests which have been proposed. For instance, it has been laid down as a "canon" that "nearly all of Chaucer's tales that are in stanzas are early, and nearly all that are in the usual [decasyllabic] couplets are late". This is a convenient generalisation which is commonly accepted, but it hardly amounts to either a test or a canon. The belief has steadily gained ground that the story of Palamon and Arcyte mentioned in the *Legende of Good Women* was practically identical with the Knight's Tale, and therefore in decasyllabic couplets, and two other Canterbury Tales in this metre, the Doctor of Physic's and the Manciple's, have been thought to be early work. On the other hand, we know that Chaucer used stanzas of seven or eight lines up to the close of his career; we know that he used the seven-line stanza for the *Parlement of Foules* as late as 1382; and curiously enough we cannot produce absolute proof of early date (*i.e.*

earlier than 1382) for any poem in this metre, though we
have good reasons for believing many of them to be early.
These good reasons depend on the tone, sources, and style
of each individual poem, and to no small extent on the
fact that Chaucer's literary life from 1379 onwards is so
crowded with poems which could only have been written
after that date that there is a reasonable presumption
that all other poems are earlier.

On these grounds, though with varying degrees of certainty, we are justified in assigning early dates, *i.e.* between 1370 and 1380, not only to the *Lyf of Seint Cecyle*,
but to the *Story of Grisilde* (Clerk's Tale), the *Story of
Constance* (Man of Law's Tale), and to a first draft of the
"Tragedies of the Great", which were afterwards revised
and added to and assigned to the jovial Monk. On the
other hand, the story of the Martyred Chorister (Prioress's
Tale), though it has been assigned to this period, is
almost certainly later.

(3) USE OF BOETHIUS.—We have seen that Chaucer's
prose translation of the *De Consolatione* was probably
written about the same time as his *Troilus, i.e.* between
1380 and 1382. The book was so popular in the Middle
Ages that we must not refuse Chaucer knowledge of it
before he took the translation in hand, but in the poems
we have good reason for placing earlier than 1380 (with
the exception of the Monk's Tale) the influence of the
De Consolatione is. not apparent, while in later works
passages inspired by it are very frequent. This is perhaps
a reason for regarding the Monk's Tale as somewhat later
than the Second Nun's, Clerk's, and Man of Law's, and
it is also a reason for attributing the five poems, the
Former Age, Fortune, Truth, Gentilesse and *Lak of
Stedfastnesse*, all of which seem written more or less under
the influence of Boethius, to the period subsequent to the
translation, a period during which Chaucer's outward

circumstances more than once caused him to need all the
consolations which philosophy could bestow.

(4) EVIDENCE OF STYLE AND POWER.—We have left
to the last, and cannot even yet treat at any length, the
most important of the internal tests of date which
Chaucer's works afford. His early poems are very beautiful, but they are sentimental and a little weak, with
hardly a trace of humour and no great power of charac-
terisation. In his later poems sentiment is replaced by a
not unkindly cynicism; his sense of the beauty of religion
has perhaps not diminished, but he himself is less religious
and grosser; his subtle humour has become infinite, and
with a few masterly strokes he portrays a character to the
life. A similar change has come over his style. His verse
has become much more closely packed, and each line
seems to convey twice as much as before. To enlarge on
these differences before we have examined the poems
individually would be unfruitful. They are mentioned
here because they come to the aid of evidence of other
kinds, which by itself might seem weak or even fanciful.
Moreover, the consistent development in Chaucer's genius
which we are able to trace when we read his poems in the
order in which evidence, mainly external, suggests that
they should be arranged, comes as a strong confirmation
of our belief that the arrangement is on the whole trust-
worthy. Let us see then at what point we have so far
arrived.

§ 40. **Summary.**—If we look back over the foregoing
sections we shall see that a date, exact or approximate,
has been suggested for all Chaucer's extant works outside the *Canterbury Tales* (some of which also have been
approximately dated), with the exception [1] of the *A B C*,

---

[1] *To Rosemounde* is a fourth exception: its tone and style, and perhaps the fact that it is found in a MS. of *Troilus and Cressida*, all point
to a date after 1380.

the *Exclamacion of the Dethe of Pite*, and the translation
of the *Roman de la Rose*, if this last is to be assigned to
Chaucer. An assertion made two hundred years after
Chaucer's death tells us that the *A B C* was written for
the use of the Duchess Blanche. But we cannot rely on
this, and have no help towards dating the poem except
its style, on the ground of which most critics regard it as
the earliest of Chaucer's extant works. We are really in
the same state of helplessness about the *Dethe of Pite*,
but the desire to connect it with the hopeless love alluded
to in the *Dethe of Blaunche* has caused it to be placed
generally between 1367 and 1372. To the present writer
it seems good enough to be later even than the second of
these dates. As regards the *Romaunt of the Rose*, those
who regard the present version as in whole or part textu-
ally Chaucer's must suppose it to have been written
before his principles of versification were fixed, *i.e.* considerably earlier than 1369. If Chaucer's version be
wholly lost or if some explanation can be accepted (*see*
§ 86) as to how his text came to be so mutilated and de-
graded, we should be inclined to bring it towards the end
of the 'seventies, partly to link it up with the *Hous of
Fame* in the same metre, partly because the manner of
the reference to it in the *Legende* does not suggest that it
was translated in Chaucer's youth. There is a general
agreement that the *A B C, Pite,* and *Romaunt* were all
written before 1380, but there is no agreement which
enables us to range them in their chronological order in
Chaucer's writings. We therefore place them by themselves in the accompanying table of his works. The other
works follow, with the dates, exact or otherwise, which
have been suggested for them, while in the last column
the chief facts of the poet's life have been jotted down,
so as to show what he was doing and how he was earning
his living at each period of his poetical career. The centre

		Influenced by or Translated from	Notes on Chaucer's Life.
Before 1380	A B C { 1366? Furnivall / 1369 Koch / After 1373 Ten Brink } Pite { 1367? Furnivall / 1370–72 Ten Brink / 1374 Koch } Romaunt of Rose? [Extant version if genuine, 1360–65? if memorised, 1370–1380]	Guillaume de Deguilleville Roman de la Rose	In the King's Household.
1369–70	Dethe of Blaunche	"Ceyx and Alcione", from Ovid, Reminiscences of Machault, and Romance de la Rose	
1370–80	Lyf of Seint Cecyle, Second Nun's Tale, usually assigned to 1374, perhaps earlier [Story of Grisilde] Clerk's Tale, after 1373 [Story of Constaunce] Man of Law's Tale ?[Twelve "Tragedies" of Great Men and Women] Monk's Tale, after 1373 Compleynt of Mars Probably towards 1380	Story from Legenda Aurea (Invocation to Blessed Virgin from Dante) Petrarch's Latin version of a tale by Boccaccio Anglo-French Chronicle of Trivet (with numerous interpolations) Partly from Boccaccio's De Casibus Virorum et Mulierum Illustrium	First Mission to Italy, 1372–73. Comptroller of Customs of Wool, 1374. Employed on diplomatic missions. Very busy and prosperous. Second Mission to Italy, 1378–79.
c. 1380	Compleynt to his Lady (A fragment) Anelida and Arcyte (Unfinished)	Partly written in Dante's terza rima Seventy lines from Boccaccio's Teseide and Statius' Thebais; rest original?	
1380–84	Boece Troilus and Cressida (1380–82, Skeat; 1383–85, Lowes)	A prose version of the De Consolatione Freely adapted from Boccaccio's Filostrato	Comptroller of Petty Customs, 1382.

Date	Writings	Sources / Influences	Biographical Events
1381	Hous of Fame (Brusendorff: before 1380, Lowes; 1383-84, Skeat)	Plan from Froissart's Temple d'Honneur (Brusendorff), also much influenced by Dante's Divina Commedia	Busy with his clerk work at the Customs.
1382	Parlement of Foules (Koch, generally accepted)	Several imitations of Dante; ll. 183-294 from Boccaccio's Teseide	Comptroller of Petty Customs, 1382.
c. 1384	{Lines to Adam Scrivener / To Rosemounde}		
1385	Palamon and Arcyte, nearly as in the Knight's Tale (1381-82, Lowes, Emerson)	Freely adapted from Boccaccio's Teseide	Allowed to appoint a permanent deputy at the Customs.
1386(-94?)	Legende of Good Women (1385, Skeat)	Ovid, Virgil, and two Latin works of Boccaccio	Knight of the Shire for Kent, 1386. Loses both his Comptrollerships, 1386. His wife dies, 1387. Sells his pension, 1388. Clerk of the King's Works, 1389.
After 1386	Canterbury Tales Prologue—Talks on Road and nineteen out of twenty-three Tales	See § 73 sqq. ..	
(Any time after 1382) 1386-89 ?	Former Age / Fortune / Truth / Gentilesse / Lak of Stedfastnesse	Boethius' De Consolatione / Boethius and Roman de la Rose / Partly suggested by Boethius / Suggested by Boethius and Roman / Suggested by Boethius	Loses his Clerkship, 1391.
1391	Astrolabe	Latin version of Arabic of Messahala	
1393	Envoy to Scogan	..	
,,?	"Compleynt of Venus"	Ballades by Sir Otes de Granson	New pension granted by Richard II. 1394.
1396	Envoy to Bukton		
1399	Compleynt to his Purs		Additional pension granted by Henry IV. 1399. Death of Chaucer, 1400.

column gives, in the briefest possible notes, the names of
the author or work upon which Chaucer drew, whether
by way of translation, paraphrase, or imitation, in writing
each of his poems.

These notes suggest the four divisions under which we
may now proceed to the detailed examination of the
poet's works. Up to the date of his return from his second
visit to Italy his work shows only the scantiest trace of
the influence of Italian literature, his debts are to French
and Latin sources. We take this as his first period, his
apprenticeship, during which he did some very beautiful
work, but had not yet found the true secret of his powers.
During the next six years, 1380–85, we have four important poems, *Troilus*, the *Hous of Fame*, the *Parlement*
and *Palamon and Arcyte*, and two minor ones, in all of
which the influence of Dante or Boccaccio is strongly
marked. This, then, is Chaucer's Italian period, and we
see its close in the *Legende of Good Women*, which he
abandoned in favour of the *Canterbury Tales*. These, it
is needless to say, enshrine Chaucer's best and most
original work, and constitute a period in themselves, a
period which begins about 1387, but of which we cannot
fix the end. One or two of the Tales are less successful
than others, but we cannot say that any of them show
signs of failing power. They represent just one-half of
Chaucer's extant work, and it is possible that he continued writing them up to the end of his life. It is more
probable, however, that the poetic impulse died away
some little time before his death and that the famous
Tales were mainly compressed into some six or seven years.
This leaves us only four poems belonging to what has
been called Chaucer's period of decline, viz., the Envoys
to Scogan and Bukton, the so-called *Compleynt of Venus*
and the *Purs*. For greater convenience of treatment we
shall include in the same chapter the fine Boethius group

(*Truth, Gentilesse,* etc.) which may have been written any time after about 1382, and head the chapter "Later Minor Poems". Chaucer's work was so good right to the end that it is pleasant to be able to avoid the use of the word "decline" in connection with any of it.

CHAPTER IV

POEMS OF CHAUCER'S FIRST PERIOD

Chaucer at Work on French and Latin Models.—1360?–1379.

Note.—In addition to the extant works belonging to this period we must assign to it three translations now lost, viz. the *Book of the Lion*, borrowed from Guillaume Machault; the *Wrecched Engendryng of Mankynde*, translated from Pope Innocent III.; and the version of "Origenes *Upon the Maudelayne*" (see § 37).

§ 41. **The "A B C".**—The *Roman de la Rose* called forth many imitations, among others a religious work by a French Cistercian, Guillaume de Deguilleville, who in the year 1330 began to write his *Pèlerinaige de la vie humaine*, to which he afterwards added a *Pèlerinaige de l'âme après mort* and a *Pèlerinaige de Jésus Christ*. The first of these three poems is sufficiently described by saying that it served John Bunyan as a Catholic model for his Protestant *Pilgrim's Progress*. At one stage of his journey the Pilgrim is sorely beset by Avarice and Gluttony, and when *Grâce-Dieu* has rescued him he implores the aid of the Blessed Virgin in a poetical prayer written according to the letters of the alphabet, so that the order of the verses might be better remembered. It is this prayer which is the original of Chaucer's poem. The French is written in stanzas of twelve octosyllabic lines, rhyming *aabaabbbabba*; Chaucer's imitation in stanzas of eight decasyllabic lines, rhyming *ababbcbc*. In the French there are two additional stanzas beginning with the contractions for *et* and *con*, which were often written at the end of the alphabet. These Chaucer omits. His opening lines are very fine:

> Al-myghty and al-merciable Queene,
>   To whom that al this world fleeth for socour
> To have relees of sinne, of sorwe and teene,
>   Glorious Virgine, of allè flourès flour,
> To thee I flee confounded in errour!
>   Help, and releeve, thou myghty debonayre,
> Have mercy on my perilous languor!
>   Venquisshed me hath my cruelle adversaire.

But despite the aid of his three rhymes, as against Deguilleville's two, he is not at his ease. He begins each stanza literally and well, but soon wanders from his original, and supplies its place rather poorly. Professor Ten Brink, whose judgment is always to be respected, placed this poem as late as about 1374, a period when he thought Chaucer was unusually religious, but in the judgment of most critics it shows early work. The unsupported assertion of Speght, in the 1602 edition of Chaucer's works, that the prayer was translated by order of the Duchess Blanche, has been already mentioned.

§ 42. **The "Exclamacion of the Dethe of Pite"**.—In this beautiful little poem Chaucer tells us that he had intended to complain to Pity against the cruelty of Love, who persecuted him for his truth. But when he ran to Pity he found her dead—although no man knew this but he—and standing about her hearse were all the qualities which release men from the need of compassion, Beauty, Jollity, Assured Manner, Youth, and their fellows, confederates in cruelty, from whom he fled. So the Complaint is never made to Pity, but he tells us the "effect" or substance of it in nine more stanzas, which bring the poem to a close. Professor Skeat supposes the idea of the personification of Pity and one or two phrases to have been taken from the ninth book of the *Thebais* of Statius. The personification of her adversaries certainly recalls the first part of the *Roman de la Rose*. But Chaucer's poem is quite independent of both works, and, especially in the eight verses which preface the Complaint, is singularly beautiful. The Complaint is not so well managed, and has sometimes been misunderstood, owing to Pity being partly confused with the lady to win whom her aid is sought. The different dates assigned to this poem have been mentioned in § 40, and the attempt to interpret it biographically in § 8. The two questions hang together, and neither can be answered with any certainty.

§ 43. **The "Romaunt of the Rose".**—An outline of both the parts of the French original of Chaucer's translation has been given in §§ 28, 29, and we shall have to consider the authorship of the extant version at some length (§ 86) While the extant fragments were regarded as Chaucer's and substantially as he wrote them they were reckoned as his earliest work. If the text is admitted to have been debased by imperfect memory they should belong to the later 'seventies.

§ 44. **"Dethe of Blaunche the Duchesse",** 1369.—In the Prologue to this poem Chaucer feigns that in default of sleep, of which by a "sickness" he has "suffred this eight year" he is bereft, he reads the story of Ceyx and Alcione, where the drowned king is sent by Juno in a dre^m to his faithful wife. A vow to Juno and Morpheus lulls the poet into a deep sleep, in which he sees the dream which forms his real subject. He dreams that he is wakened one May morning by the song of birds. The windows of his room are painted with the stories of Troy, and the walls with the *Romaunt of the Rose*. He hears horns, takes horse, and finds the Emperor Octavian is hunting. He strays by himself and at last is ware of a man in black, a fair knight

of four-and-twenty years,[1] seated under an oak lamenting.
He asks him of his sorrow (for to tell a trouble eases the
heart), and the knight complains of Fortune who has
played with him as at chess with false pieces and stolen
his "fers" or "queen". Since he has had understanding he
has been Love's tributary, and one day it happened to
him to come into a company of fair ladies and there to see
the fairest of all, the "goode faire *White*", so by translation he calls her, whose beauty and goodness he describes
at great length. On her all his love was laid, to see her in
the morn healed his sorrows for all the day, and for per-
plexity how to tell his love his heart almost "brast
a-tweyn". When he spoke he was answered "Nay", but
another year's waiting brought its reward, and we have
this lovely picture of the chivalrous ideal of marriage:

> For trewély that swetè wyght
> Whan I had wrong and she the ryght,
> She wolde alway so goodély
> Forgeve me so debonairely!
> In al my youthe, in allè chaunce
> She tooke me in hir governaunce.
> Therwyth she was alway so trewe
> Our joye was ever y-lýchè newe,
> Our hertès were so evene a payre
> That never was that oon contrayre
> To that other, for no wo;
> For sothe y-liche they suffred tho
> Oo blysse, and eke oo sorwe bothe;
> Y-lyche they were bothe glad and wrothe,
> Al was as oon withoutè were.
> And thus we lyved ful many a yeere,
> So wel, I kan nat tellè how.

With some unnecessary questioning it is made clear that
it is for the loss of this peerless wife that the knight
laments. "Is that your losse? By God, it is routhe," is the
comment, and then the King (as the "Emperor Octavian",

---

[1] At the time of his wife's death John of Gaunt was twenty-nine. It
has been suggested that a copyist may have mistaken xxix. for xxiv.

i.e. Edward III., is now called) is seen returning from the
hunt to his "long castle with walles whyte" (Windsor?),
and as a bell strikes noon the poet awakes and determines
"by process of time" to put his dream into verse.

The *Dethe of Blaunche* is not, as a French critic rashly
asserted, a "mere servile imitation of Machault". The
incident of Ceyx and Alcione is taken direct from Ovid,
though Chaucer had probably also seen the *Dit de la Fon-
taine Amoureuse* in which Machault imitated the same
passage. To Machault's *Remède de Fortune* and to the
Roman de la Rose Chaucer is certainly under obligations,
though not very great ones. But while his poem is original
in substance, it cannot be called original in form. The
dream, the May morning, the fair park full of singing-
birds, all these are from the French, and the poem shares
also the discursiveness of its models. Isolated passages
in it are fine, but it is hardly fine as a whole. Even the
justly praised portrait of the knight's lady is rather an
assemblage of fair qualities than a real character.

In § 8 something has already been said as to the poet's
reference to his own eight-years' "sickness" in the opening lines, and we need not allude to it further here.

§ 45. **The "Lyf of Seint Cecyle" (Second Nun's Tale).**—
We have had already to allude to this tale several times
(§§ 38, 39), and have noted its mention in the Prologue to
the *Legende of Good Women*, and subsequent appearance in
the Canterbury Pilgrimage as the tale of the Second Nun,
who is made to narrate it without any alteration of the
allusions (i.) to the teller as a "son" instead of a daughter
"of Eve", and (ii.) to the story having been written for
readers instead of spoken to an audience. In the *Canterbury Tales* also it is preceded by no conversation between
the host and the nun, and this is another sign that it was
never finally revised for its present position. Instead of
this talk we have a prologue on the sin of idleness, the

suggestion (not the phrasing) of which Chaucer seems to
have taken from a similar prologue to Jehan de Vignay's
French translation of the *Legenda Aurea*, though in the
tale itself he follows the original Latin and not the French
version. This prologue leads up to an Invocation to the
Blessed Virgin Mary, about a fourth of which imitates
closely part of the first twenty-one lines of Dante's *Paradiso*, cant. xxxiii., or, as has also been suggested, "their
original in some Latin prayer or hymn". The tale is
further prefaced, as in the *Legenda*, by an attempted
"interpretation of the name Cecilia", on the basis of
various impossible etymologies. Thenceforward it is un-
interrupted, and we read of Cecilia's conversion of her
husband Valerian by aid of a miracle, of the effect of her
constancy on her persecutors, of the boiling bath heated
day and night for ten days and yet cool to her, and finally
of the three sword-strokes on her neck, which nevertheless allowed her to live and comfort her fellow-Christians
for three days. It is expressly mentioned that "whan toold
was al the lyf of Seinte Cecile", the pilgrims were nearing
Boughton-under-Blee, so that there can be no doubt that
Chaucer intended to give it a place among the *Tales*,
without, however, finally revising it for this purpose. But
though the *Lyf* was never thus finally revised, and though
the Prologue and Invocation and the story itself are all
written in the same seven-lined stanza, it is not certain
that they were all written at the same time. The tale,
despite some judicious omissions on Chaucer's part, is
rather poorly told, whereas the verse of the Prologue and
Invocation is strong and free, and it is at least possible
that it represents a later addition made some time before
1385. If this view be accepted, we shall date the *Lyf* itself
as early as we can, *i.e.* about 1370; otherwise it must be
placed soon after Chaucer's first visit to Italy, in 1373 or
1374.

§ 46. **The "Story of Grisilde" (Clerk's Tale).**—In the story of Grisilde Chaucer tells us how an Italian marquis chose one of his subjects, a good and beautiful peasant girl, for his wife, first making her promise to obey him in all things. In her new life she bore herself with such wisdom and sweet dignity that all men praised her; but a strange passion seized the marquis to test to the uttermost her promised obedience. He pretended that his people scorned to be ruled over by the children of a peasant, and caused her to give up first her baby daughter and then her little son, as if to be killed. Then he sent her away, saying he would take another wife, and one day bade her return to make ready the palace for the new marchioness. When the bride arrived he asked Grisilde what she thought of her, and Grisilde praised her kindly, but besought one thing:

> That ye ne prikkė with no tórmentinge
> This tendrė mayden, as ye han doon mo.[1]

And this was the nearest word to a reproach she ever uttered. The pretended bride turns out to be her own daughter, the bride's brother her son, and with words of praise Grisilde is welcomed once more to her old position, which she meekly accepts. If we keep our eyes fixed on utter and unrepining obedience as the one quality which Grisilde had to exemplify, we shall find the story full of tender beauty. If we judge it as we should a modern story, it becomes hateful and impossible, as some people found the Italian version even in Chaucer's day. This Italian version was made by Boccaccio and recited to his friend Petrarch, who had heard the story many years before, and was now moved to write it down in Latin, keeping to Boccaccio's incidents, but moralising and amplifying his narrative. Chaucer's poem, for the most part, follows Petrarch very closely, though he adds a few

---

[1] *Mo*, more, others.

vivid touches of his own, and expands some of the pathetic parts very considerably. When he came to use it as one of the *Canterbury Tales* he assigned it to the Clerk of Oxenford, and makes him say distinctly that he learnt it at Padua of a worthy clerk, "Fraunceys Petrark, the laureat poete". Now as we have noted (§ 12), Petrarch's letter to Boccaccio, which follows on this story, is dated in some copies, 8th June 1373. In the spring of this year, 1373, Chaucer was in the north of Italy; and if he visited Petrarch, who from November 1372 to September 1373 (he died in June 1374) was residing at Padua, we can understand how he became possessed of a manuscript of the tale, while it is not very easy to imagine how else it is likely to have fallen in his way. So that on the whole it is best to believe that what he wrote of his Clerk of Oxenford he meant to be taken of himself, and that he actually did visit Petrarch and heard from him the story of Grisilde. If so, we shall not be far wrong in placing the date of Chaucer's version about the year 1374, *i.e.* very soon after his return from his first mission to Italy. By the time he wrote it he had gained considerable ease in the use of the seven-line stanza, and his translation (though he sometimes makes mistakes) is often as close to his original as if he were writing in prose. When he revised the poem for insertion in the *Canterbury Tales* he tacked on two stanzas and an envoy of thirty-six lines (rhyming throughout *ababcb*), in which he satirised all "arche-wyves", and it was probably at this time also that he inserted two stanzas (ll. 995-1008), beginning:

O stormy peple ! unsad and ever untrewe !

in which he scorns the fickleness of the mob. In 1374 his views both of women and of mobs were as yet unembittered.

§ 47. " Story of Constance " (Man of Law's Tale).—The

story of Constance illustrates the Christian virtue of
Fortitude as that of Grisilde the Christian virtue of
Obedience; and by the modern reader it must be read
with the same mindfulness of the standpoint from which
it was written. Daughter of an Emperor of Rome, Constance is given in marriage to a Soldan as a condition of
his conversion. By the wickedness of his mother the
Soldan is killed and Constance thrust out to sea in a little
boat. By a miracle she is preserved for three years, and
at last reaches the coast of Britain, and there converts
the "Constable" of the place where she lands, and finally
the King, Alla, who marries her. But Alla's mother,
during his absence, procures that she shall once more be
sent to sea in her open boat, this time with her babe in
her arms, and after another five years' voyage she is
picked up by a Roman vessel and eventually restored to
both her father and her husband. There are many blots
in the story: the monotony of the parts played by the
two mothers-in-law—one in Syria, the other in North-
umberland—the unreasoning prodigality of time, and
the refusal of Constance to declare who she is, being the
most obvious. Chaucer had not so good material to work
on as in the tale of Grisilde, and he had not yet learnt to
reconstruct a story for himself, or to clothe his characters
in flesh and blood. His authority was the Anglo-French
chronicle of Nicholas Trivet, a Dominican friar, educated
in London, Oxford, and Paris, who wrote nearly a score
of commentaries and expositions on authors popular in
the Middle Ages, and annals and chronicles both of the
world before Christ and of his own time. He died probably soon after 1334. Chaucer took his facts from Trivet,
though he deliberately alters them in one or two small
points; but he uses his own language, abridges freely, and
while he takes something under 700 lines from his author,
he adds about 350 of his own. These 350 lines are all by

way of poetic embellishments, exclamations, moralisings, and descriptions, and they show that Chaucer was becoming increasingly conscious both of his own powers and of what was required by his art. The added lines constitute the very salt of the poem, including as they do the mother's beautiful words of pity to her innocent babe and the two notable speeches of the Soldaness to her friends. We should note also the stanzas on the influence of the stars (ll. 190-203, 295-315), and the first appearance of Chaucer's humour in such phrases as

> Housbondes been allé good and han been yoore;
> That knowen wyves, I dar say yow na moore.

And the

> Coold water shall nat greeve us but a lite,

of the Soldaness's reference to Holy Baptism.

In § 37 we have already noted the appearance in different places in this poem of altogether seven and a half stanzas derived from the treatise *De Miseria Conditionis Humanae* of Pope Innocent III. Whether any of these additions to Trivet's story were made by Chaucer subsequently to the first draft of his poem it is impossible to say; but the poet's obvious desire to improve his original, and the free movement of his stanzas, are in rather striking contrast to the poverty of his plot and characters, and make it difficult to guess about what year the story could have been written. Its ascription in the *Canterbury Tales* to the Man of Law has no appropriateness, and this confirms our opinion that it was not originally written for him. But if we are right in assigning it to the period before 1380, we must assign it to as late in that period as possible.

§ 48. **Twelve "Tragedies" in the Monk's Tale.**—A difficulty similar to that expressed in the last paragraph meets us when we try to fix a date for twelve of the seven-

teen "tragedies" or stories of the misfortunes of great men
and women, which are assigned to the Monk in the
Canterbury Tales. Four of these tragedies deal with
modern subjects, the rest with ancient; and as the four
hang together, and one of them celebrates the death of
Bernabo Visconti, Lord of Milan, in 1385, we may be sure
that these were written when the scheme of the *Canterbury Tales* was already conceived. The same may be said
of the last story, that of Crœsus, which obviously leads
up to the rebuke with which the Monk is "stinted" of his
tale. The remaining twelve tragedies tell the stories of
Lucifer, Adam, Samson, Hercules, Nebuchadnezzar,
Belshazzar, Zenobia, Nero, Holofernes, Antiochus, Alex-
ander, and Julius Cæsar, in an order in which chronological sequence is only disturbed by a little appropriate
pairing, and by Nero and Zenobia being taken out of
their right positions in order the better to cover the insertion of the four stories of the thirteenth and fourteenth
centuries which are placed between them. One of the
modern stories, that of Ugolino of Pisa, is partly taken
from Dante, and is strikingly better than all the rest. In
the early stories, though the verse is good enough, the
treatment is often careless and unsympathetic, and
Chaucer was clearly not interested in them. It cannot be
said dogmatically that they show early work, but it
seems probable that at some time towards the close of
the period with which we are now dealing (1369–1379)
Chaucer began a poem on the same plan afterwards
adopted by his follower Lydgate for his *Falls of Princes*,
and then abandoned it, till the need came to suit the
Monk with an unexpected but appropriate theme. The
Bible, Boccaccio's *De Casibus Virorum et Feminarum
Illustrium* and *De Claris Mulieribus*, Boethius and the
Roman de la Rose, furnished the materials for these
twelve tales, and they give us practically no help towards

dating them. But if Chaucer wrote all seventeen tragedies about 1386 it is hard to believe that he would not have made something better out of them, or, if the stopping of the Monk was in his view from the first, would not have brought this about more amusingly. As it is, he seems first to have tried to better his old work by adding to it, and then to have given up the attempt in despair, and turned his own failure into ridicule. The metre is the same eight-line stanza used in the *A B C*. And perhaps this favours an early date for most of the poem as may also the treat-ment in the lines on Julius Cæsar of " Brutus Cassius" as one person.

§ 49. " **The Compleynt of Mars.**"—*The Compleynt of Mars* is founded on the old mythological story, told by Ovid in *Metam.* iv. 170-189, of the love of the god Mars for the goddess Venus, and its discovery by Phœbus Apollo. This story Chaucer here works out, according to the astronomy of the day, of a conjunction of the planet Mars with the planet Venus in the sign of Taurus, or the Bull, one of the two astrological "houses" of Venus, into which Phœbus, or the Sun, enters every year on 12th April. If we may trust two notes of the copyist Shirley in a MS. in Trinity College, Cambridge, this astrological myth is also an allegory made "at the commandment of the renowned and excellent prince my lord the Duke John of Lancaster", and "as some men say . . . by [*i.e.* concerning] my lady of York, daughter to the King of Spain, and my lord of Huntingdon, sometime Duke of Exeter". We must note that Shirley makes his statement only as a piece of gossip, and no other confirmation has been found for it than (i.) a hint by the chronicler-monk Walsingham that the Lady Isabella had not always led a good life, and (ii.) an in-genious supposition of Professor Skeat's that three stanzas in the poem which treat of the "Brooch of Thebes" may contain a punning allusion to a tablet of jasper, which we know from her will that Isabella was given by the King of Armenia. The first owner of the Theban brooch, which all men desired and none obtained save to their undoing, was Harmonia, daughter of Mars and Venus, and it only received the name of the "Brooch of Thebes" from the special mischief it wrought that city. Harmonia and Armenia might both in Middle English be written "Armonye", and a far-fetched pun, quite in keeping with the poem, is thus at least possible. Even thus strengthened, Shirley's bit of gossip does not command very great respect, for a poem on such a subject was sure in any case to find malevolent interpreters, and the poet's interest is so plainly in the stars that it is difficult to accept the theory that the whole poem is an unpleasant allegory. If we reject Shirley's gossip we may revive Dr. Koch's arguments, noticed in § 38, and imagine that in 1379, when Mars, Venus, and the Sun were nearly, though not quite, in the positions described, Chaucer may have been reminded of Ovid's story, and have written this curious medley of astronomy and mythology, without any court intrigue or unbrotherly suggestion of John of Gaunt's to spur him on. The point cannot be settled, and is only of antiquarian interest.

The first 154 lines of the poem are written in seven-line stanzas, and, as we are told in ll. 13, 14, are supposed to be spoken by a bird before sunrise on St. Valentine's Day. Beginning with a little song, he tells the story of Mars and Venus, and of the comforting of Venus by Mercury, setting forth every detail with minute astronomical accuracy, even to such a precise but ungallant observation as that Venus hurried to meet Mars twice as fast as he to her. Then we have the "Compleynt of Mars" from which the poem takes its name. This consists of a prosaic prelude, followed by fifteen stanzas divided by their subjects into five sections of three stanzas each. The themes of the several sections are as follows: (i.) The lover's devotion; (ii.) his lady is sick at heart; (iii.) Love brings woe oftener than the moon changes; (iv.) it is like the "Brooch of Thebes", ever desired, ever bringing sorrow on its possessor; (v.) all knights, ladies, and lovers should sympathise with Mars. Without doubt the poem is very clever and ingenious, but it is not one of Chaucer's masterpieces; nor, if Shirley's story be true, did it deserve to be. The incident of the "Brooch of Thebes" is found in Statius, *Thebais* ii. 265 *sqq.*, and it was probably there that Chaucer read about it.

§ 50. **Chaucer's Late Development.**—In this chapter we have considered only eight out of some fifty poems written by Chaucer. Of these eight poems the four usually printed among his Minor Works, *i.e.* the *A B C*, the *Dethe of Pite*, the *Dethe of the Duchesse*, and the *Compleynt of Mars*, contain altogether 1935 lines. The other four poems are taken from among the *Canterbury Tales*: one, the *Lyf of Seint Cecyle*, on Chaucer's own authority; another, the story of Grisilde, with strong probability; the third and fourth, the story of Constance and the twelve Tragedies from the Monk's Tale, rather doubtfully. These four excerpts from the *Canterbury Tales* give us another 3378 lines, or a grand total of 5313 lines to represent the whole of Chaucer's poetry in, roughly speaking, the first forty years of his life—so far as we now have it. The poems generally accepted as written by Chaucer contain altogether nearly 35,000 lines, so that we have the very uneven division of a little under 30,000 lines of verse, in addition to four prose works, written between forty and sixty, and only a little over 5000 lines of verse written up to the age of forty—one-seventh of Chaucer's extant work written in the prime of life; sixth-sevenths in middle age!

A note at the beginning of this chapter has already reminded us of the loss of three translations by Chaucer probably made during this period. These and a fourth translation, that of the *Roman de la Rose*, if all were now extant, might conceivably bring the work of the two periods very nearly equal in point of quantity. It is reasonable to suppose that Chaucer began at the beginning of the *Roman*—many scholars believe that we have at least 1700 lines of his version of the first part still extant. We know from himself that he translated at least some of the second part, that continuation by Jean de Meung which Love reckoned as a heresy against his law. As we have seen (§§ 28, 29), there are about 22,000 lines in the two parts of the *Roman*, and if Chaucer ever had the patience to translate them all we need not wonder that he found leisure for very little other poetry. It is not likely that he had this patience, but the *Roman* may have been worked at desultorily over many years and its loss helps to explain why this period of his life appears so unproductive. The main reason is that Chaucer was busy in these days in making his way, and his poetry could not do much for him. Queen Philippa was dead, Edward III. in his dotage; there was only John of Gaunt to look to, and John of Gaunt, though he may have set Chaucer to write poetry, once, twice, or thrice, as critics choose to imagine, probably valued him more as a man of action than as a man of letters. It was by service in the King's Court, on diplomatic missions, and at the Custom-House that a living had to be earned and a substantial position won; and it is to these objects, trivial in his case as we may now think them, that Chaucer appears to have devoted the best years of his life. If we had only the quantity of his verse to judge by, we should hardly, in our uncertainty as to how much has been lost, be entitled to speak thus; but we have also the much more decisive test of quality. If Shakespeare had

died in his thirtieth year who could have guessed that
he had it in him to write *Hamlet* and *King Lear*? From
the very outset Chaucer was introducing new themes and
new music into English poetry, but his early work was
thin, and the charm of a few hundred lines in the *Dethe
of Blaunche* and the pathos of the stories of *Grisilde* and
Constance are the chief titles to remembrance of all the
poems he wrote on the younger side of forty. From the
very first he is distinguished from his contemporaries by
the music of his verse; but the humour, the insight into
character, the knowledge of life, the entire mastery of
words, the essential qualities, that is, which we now
connect with his name, all came to Chaucer exceptionally
late.

CHAPTER V

POEMS OF CHAUCER'S SECOND PERIOD—CHAUCER AT WORK ON ITALIAN MODELS

§ 51. **"Palamon and Arcyte"** (*lost?*).—In § 37 attention
has already been called to the mention in Chaucer's list of
his works in the *Legende of Good Women* of a story containing "al the love of Palamon and Arcyte". As then
pointed out, the fragmentary lines (closely translated
from Boccaccio's *Teseide*) which are at present dove-
tailed into *Anelida and Arcyte*, the *Parlement of Foules*,
and *Troilus*, have led some scholars to think that this
Palamon and Arcyte is not the story told in heroic couplets in the Knight's Tale, but an earlier version written
in stanzas, and afterwards suppressed, odd verses being
used up in the poems named. If this be so, the lost version of *Palamon and Arcyte* is necessarily earlier than
any of the poems in which use is made of it, *i.e.* is necessarily earlier than 1382 (date of the *Parlement of Foules*).
My own belief, however, is that no such poem was ever

written, and that the allusion is to that which we now know as the Knight's Tale.

§ 52. "Compleynt to his Lady."—The 117 lines to which the title *A Compleynt to his Lady* has been assigned consist of four fragments in three different metres. In the Harleian MS. 78 (by Shirley), and in Stowe's edition of 1561 in which the lines were first printed (not from Shirley's copy), they are tacked on to the *Exclamacion of the Dethe of Pite*, which is, however, complete without them. The first fragment consists of two seven-line stanzas, the next of eight lines rhyming *a, zab, abc, b*, a metrical system which the seventeen lines which follow, rhyming *zab, abc, bcd, cde, def, ef* . . ., show to be the first of two attempts in Dante's *terza rima*. The fourth fragment consists of eight stanzas (the second imperfect), each of ten decasyllabic lines, rhyming *aab, aab, cd, dc*. In the first fragment the poet tells us how he cannot sleep, "so desespeired I am from allè blisse"; in the second "the more I love the more she doth me smerte"; in the third he asks

> Now hath not Lovè me bestowed weel
> To lovè, ther I never shal have part?

and complains

> I can but love hir best, my swetè fo;
> Love hath me taught no more of his art
> But serve alwey, and stintè for no wo.

The last and longest fragment begins with a variation of a lament which occurs also in the *Pite* (ll. 99-104) and *Parlement of Foules* (ll. 90, 91):

> For al that thing which I desyre I mis,
> And al that ever I woldè not, i-wis
> That fynde I redy to me evermore.

And, after many protestations, ends with the cry that, if no truer servant can be found and the poet yet be suffered to die for no guilt save his goodwill, "as good were thanne untrewe as trewe to be".

A poem which consists only of a series of fragments is necessarily difficult to date. There are strong resemblances to the *Pite*, and Dr. Koch, who dates that poem about 1373-74, naturally assigns this *Compleynt* to the same period. But the lines quoted above connect it equally with the *Parlement of Foules*, and there are some resemblances also to phrases in *Anelida and Arcyte*, and a common interest in metrical experiments. Even at the risk of having to assign a later date to the *Pite* than has yet been proposed, it seems best to place this *Compleynt* about the year 1380. There is no good reason for endeavouring to extract from it any biographical references.

§ 53. **"Anelida and Arcyte."**—Like the *Compleynt to his Lady*, this poem is of great interest metrically. It consists of an Invocation and story in thirty seven-line stanzas, followed by a *Compleynt* very artfully constructed of fourteen stanzas arranged in a Prelude, two strophes or movements of six stanzas each, and a Conclusion. The prelude, conclusion, and first four stanzas of each strophe are each of nine decasyllabic lines, rhyming *aab*, *aab*, *bab*. The fifth stanzas consist of two parts, each of eight lines, the fourth and eighth lines having ten syllables, the other lines only eight. The rhymes in the first part run *aaab*, *aaab*, and in the second part the same rhymes are taken up and reversed, *bbba*, *bbba*. In the two last stanzas of the strophes a fresh variation is obtained by an internal rhyme on the fourth and eighth syllables being introduced into the nine-line stanza in which the greater part of the poem is written. Only the professed student of Chaucer's metres need concern himself with the exact details of these variations, but the general result from them is not unimportant. We have noted above how hampered by his metre Chaucer appears in his *A B C*, and we now find him delighting to dance in fetters, writing stanzas of sixteen lines with only two rhymes in them, and turning from these to introduce internal rhymes into a nine-line stanza already sufficiently complicated. One or two of the rhymes are not quite as easy as Chaucer's usually are, but there is no other sign of distress, and both his greater skill and his greater interest in metrical experiments deserve noting.

Turning from the form of *Anelida and Arcyte* to its subject we find that we have first an invocation to Mars and the Muse Polyhymnia, followed by a story as to the source of which Chaucer tells us, "First folow I Stace and after him Corinne". The reference to Statius is justified by a few lines taken from the *Thebais*. As to "Corinne" we are told that there was a Greek Corinna, and possibly a Greek Corinnus, writers of works, now lost, which Chaucer could certainly never have construed. A conjecture by Dr. E. F. Shannon in his *Chaucer and the Roman Poets* (1929) cleverly explains the name as a reference by a mediaeval title to Ovid's *Amores*, yet it seems used to cover the stanzas here borrowed from Boccaccio's *Teseide*, just as in *Troilus and Criseyde* the name Lollius seems to cover the use of Boccaccio's *Filostrato*—the reason of the mystery being in each case obscure. These four stanzas from the *Teseide* with which the poem opens describe the entry of Theseus into Athens after his campaign in Scythia. We know from the Knight's Tale, in which Chaucer translated the same passage, sometimes in the same words, that Theseus was then met by ladies from Thebes complaining of the cruelty of Creon, its tyrant, in leaving unburied the bodies of their husbands slain in battle. In the Knight's Tale Theseus immediately rides off and defeats Creon, and captures both the Theban knight Arcyte and his friend Palamon. We can thus see the point to which Chaucer meant to work round, but in the present poem he leaves

Theseus riding to Athens in l. 46, and though we have
300 more lines of the story extant we do not even
approach an explanation of why Theseus is dragged in.
These 300 lines are occupied by a description of Arcyte's
faithless love for Anelida, and of his desertion of her for
another lady, who treats him as harshly as he deserves.
After this comes the *Compleynt*, written by Anelida with
her own hand, and sent to her false knight. Following the
Compleynt we have only one more stanza (not in all the
MSS.), and then the poem breaks off. We may imagine
that some hundreds of lines further on Theseus was meant
to appear and avenge Anelida on the cruel Arcyte, but
his introduction at the outset, so long before he is wanted,
remains inartistic. Doubtless it may be held that this was
at least partly due to Chaucer's desire to use up some
stanzas of his hypothetical *Palamon and Arcyte*, just as
the reference to the Temple of Mars in the last verse of
the poem gives us a hint that he was intending to use
another passage from the *Teseide*, which afterwards appeared in the Knight's Tale.

Professor Skeat pointed out that a line in *Anelida and
Arcyte* (237) is repeated from *A Compleynt to his Lady*
(l. 50), and that there are other resemblances. Like the
fragmentary *Compleynt*, the unfinished *Anelida* is difficult
to date; but it seems probable that it represents Chaucer's
first study of the *Teseide* before he turned to the *Filostrato*, and should thus be placed immediately before
Troilus and Criseyde, *i.e.* about 1380. It should be noted
that for four-fifths of the poem as we have it, *i.e.* all the
part which tells us of Anelida, no original has been found.

§ 54. **"Boece."**—The *De Consolatione Philosophiae* is
a treatise in five books, each book being divided into
sections, written alternately in prose or verse. Its author
was the Roman Senator Boethius, cruelly murdered in
A.D. 525 by order of his master, Theodoric, King of the

Goths. In his youth and early manhood Boethius had been a diligent student of Greek science and philosophy, and had translated and annotated some of the chief Greek treatises on mathematics, mechanics, music, logic, and theology. But in obedience to the theory laid down by Plato in his *Republic*, that public office is a burden which the good man, and especially the philosopher, should undertake for the advantage of the State, Boethius took part in politics, gained the favour of King Theodoric, and was appointed Consul for the year A.D. 510. In A.D. 522 his influence was at its height, and against all precedent the Consulship was divided between his two sons, purely out of compliment to their illustrious father. Three years later Boethius ventured to protest against a tyrannical prosecution directed against a fellow-senator by his master. He was hurried away from his luxurious palace and his beloved books and imprisoned at Pavia, where he was finally tortured to death. During his imprisonment he wrote his treatise on the *Consolation of Philosophy*, a work which though now little read is still mentioned with respect for the beauty of its style, and throughout the Middle Ages was regarded as a storehouse of noble thought.

Boethius imagines himself visited in his imprisonment by his divine mistress, Philosophy, who listens to the story of his troubles and to his complaints against his unjust accusers, and then proceeds to apply her remedies. These are at first the "lighter medecines" afforded by such topics as the proverbial inconstancy of Fortune, the sufferer's past prosperity, and the blessings that still remain to him in the well-being of his wife and sons. Not riches, nor honour, nor power, nor fame constitute true happiness, but this is found in obedience to the law of love which governs all things. Then Philosophy begins to apply her "severer" and "more pungent" remedies, and the deceitfulness of all the tests of happiness on which men rely is shown from a fresh standpoint. Hence we rise to the idea of God Himself as the Supreme Good, the rule and square of things desirable, the haven of rest, and pass on to consider the problems of the existence of evil, the rewards of virtue and vice, and the reconciliation of man's freewill with God's foreknowledge. All these points are really treated from the standpoint of the Stoics, but the Christianity of Boethius was taken for granted in the Middle Ages, and he was even credited with the composition of various treatises against heresy. The prose in which the arguments of Philosophy are expressed in the *De Consolatione* is diversified by a succession of short poems or "metres", in which similar lessons are taught, often by analogies drawn from the forces of Nature. Chaucer's translation is wholly in prose, which seldom runs very fluently, and is at times obscure. But the task-work of this prose version left him profoundly influenced by Boethius, and in many of the poems composed while he was at work on it, and in subsequent years, notably in *Troilus*, the Knight's Tale, and the fine series of poems entitled the *Former Age, Fortune, Lak of Stedfast-nesse, Gentilesse*, and *Truth*, we find paraphrases and expansions of ideas which occur in the *De Consolatione* and even, as in *Troilus*, Bk. v. ll. 963-1059 (the argument on Freewill), a close imitation of long passages.

The exceptional number of passages imitated from the *De Consolatione* in Chaucer's *Troilus*, and the mention of the poem and the translation together in the *Lines to Adam Scrivener*, suggest that the two works were in hand about the same time. Probably the translation was slightly the earlier of the two. We cannot date it more exactly than about 1380-82.

§ 55. "**Troilus and Criseyde.**"—This is the longest and most ambitious of Chaucer's extant poems, and he may have taken proportionately long in writing and rewriting it. In a miniature prefixed to the MS. at Corpus Christi College, Cambridge, he is shown reading aloud in the garden of a castle to a courtly audience. It is possible, though unlikely, that he may have told the story to amuse such an audience early enough to account for the dream of Somnolent in Gower's *Mirour de l'Omme* (finished *c.* 1379), "qu'il oït chanter la geste De Tröylus et de la belle Criseyde". On the other hand, if the poem was written straight on, and we follow Professor Lowes in finding an allusion to Queen Anna in line 171 *sq.*, "Right as our firste lettre is now an A, In beauté first so stood she makeles", it must be dated after January 1382.

The exact number of lines in the *Troilus* is 8246, and according to Mr. W. M. Rossetti's careful estimate 5663 of these are due to Chaucer alone (save in so far that he took something over a hundred of them from Petrarch, Boethius, and Dante). The remaining 2582 lines are condensed from 2730 of Boccaccio's *Filostrato*, a poem which contains in all 5704. Disregarding figures, then, we may say that Chaucer rejected more than one-half of the poem from which he was borrowing, and added to what he took considerably more than twice as much of his own.

Cressida or Criseyde is ultimately the fair Briseis, the captive of Achilles, and the innocent occasion of his great wrath, which forms the subject of the *Iliad*. But in the Middle Ages Homer was only a name, and the first germ of the story of which she is now the faithless heroine seems to be found in the string of favourable epithets with which she is mentioned by Dares Phrygius (§ 26). To Benoît de Sainte Maur (§ 25) she owes her development. He first tells how her father Calchas, having left her behind when he deserted the Trojans, persuaded the Greeks to exchange the Trojan prince, Antenor, against her; how she was escorted to the

Greek camp by Diomede, who wellnigh persuaded her to forget her earlier Trojan love, Troilus; then how Troilus wounded Diomede almost to the death, and Briseida (so Benoît calls her) in pity for Diomede's wound at last gave herself wholly over to him. When Boccaccio took up the story he retold it from the side of Troilus, made Briseida —who is now called Griseida—a widow instead of a maid, and invented the character of her-cousin, Pandarus, the bosom friend of Troilus. To his poem, which is written like his *Teseide* in eight-line stanzas, he gave the name *Filostrato, i.e.* Philostratus, which he imagined to mean, not, as it does, lover of warfare, but "love-vanquished". Chaucer further altered the story in two ways. He made Pandarus an older man, the uncle, instead of the cousin, of Criseyde, and invested him with a great deal of humour and worldly wisdom. Criseyde herself, at least during her stay in Troy, he raised and refined in every possible manner, so much so, indeed, that, as Mr. Rossetti rightly remarks, her subsequent treachery to Troilus becomes much less intelligible than it is in Boccaccio.

Despite occasional prolixity and a few artistic flaws *Troilus and Criseyde* is perhaps the most beautiful poem of its kind in the English language. Yet Chaucer, speaking in his own person as a Christian man, in three stanzas of very great beauty condemns the theory of life and love that underlies it. This theory is that of most of the romances of chivalry, and we may catch a glimpse of it by remembering the story of Grisilde, and, again, Chaucer's phrase, "the seintes legendes of Cupide" (*i.e.* the Legends of Cupid's Saints), for his stories of the women who have died for love. If Patience could be so isolated from all other virtues as to make it praiseworthy in Griselde to consent to the murder of her children, it is small wonder that Love also was erected into a religion with its own code of morality. We shall be mistaken, indeed, if we

think that this code was either an easy or a base one. To
be-a good lover a knight had to be brave unto death,
courteous to all men, humble to his lady, pure of thought,
modest of speech, ready to sacrifice all, even his love
itself, for his lady's honour. Whom he loved was reckoned
a matter of destiny, and this was held to excuse all. The
attractions of such a theory are not dead yet, but it
ignores some of the elementary facts of human nature, and
while worldly folk smile cynically at its impracticability
Religion has never wavered in its strenuous condemnation. In taking farewell of their readers Boccaccio is the
spokesman of the World, Chaucer of Religion: "O yonge
fresshe folkes", he writes:

> O yongè fresshè folkès, he or she,
> In which ay love up-groweth with youre age,
> Repeireth hom fro worldly vanyte,
> And of youre herte up-casteth the visage
> To thilkè God, that after his ymage
> You made, and thynketh al nys but a faire,
> This world that passeth soon, as flourès faire.
>   And loveth Hym, the which that right for love
> Upon a cros, our soulès for to beye,
> First starf, and roos, and sitt in heven above,
> For he nyl falsen no wight, dar I seye,
> That wol his herte alle hoolly on hym leye;
> And syn he best to love is, and most meke,
> What nedeth feynèd lovès for to seke?

Late in his life Chaucer is said to have repented that he
ever wrote this story; that he ever wrote anything, in
fact, save lives of the saints and prose treatises of philosophy. Few sane people will share this view. *Troilus and
Criseyde* is not good for all men to read, nor for any man
at the wrong age or season, but it is written by a great
poet who knew the troubles and temptations of life, and
thought about them while he was writing it; and no poem
so written, in the sum of its influence, can be otherwise
than good.

Only a detailed study of the *Filostrato* reveals by how much Chaucer has ennobled the characters both of hero and heroine. In his hands Troilus becomes a type of faithful self-sacrificing love according to the ideal of chivalry; Criseyde, the sweetest, most piteous of unfaithful women, so that he writes of her himself:

> Ne me ne list this sely womman chyde
> Ferther than this storië wol devyse;
> Hire name, allas! is publyshėd so wyde,
> That for hire gilte it ought ynough suffise;
> And if I might excuse hire any wyse,
> For she so sory was for hire untrouthe,
> I-wis I wold excuse hire yet for routhe.

To ennoble the others the character of Pandarus is deepened and worsened. He is no longer a passionate youth, but a man of the world, using at times the language of "Cupid's Saints", but knowing exactly what he is about in helping his friend. His humour is endless, but it is not always pleasant, and he is only redeemed by his capacity for friendship.

Of the beauty of special passages in the poem it is impossible here to speak. Mr. T. H. Ward has quoted some of the best in his *English Poets* (vol. i.), and these should be read.

§ 56. **"Lines to Adam Scrivener" and "To Rosemounde".**—As mentioned above, the *Troilus* is joined to the *Boece* not only by the large number of quotations from the *De Consolatione* in the former work, but also by the little seven-line poem entitled *Chaucer's Woordes unto his owne Scriveyn*. This is so short and gives so vivid a picture of the ill-treatment authors received from their scribes that it may be quoted in full, despite the unpleasant humour of the third line. "Adam Scriveyn", it runs:

> Adam Scriveyn, if ever it thee befalle
> Boece or Troylus for to writė newe,
> Under thy lockės maist thou have the scalle,

But after my making thou writė trewe:
So oft a day I mote thy werke renewe,
It to correct and eke to rubbe and scrape;
And all is thurgh thy necgligence and rape.[1]

The date of this remonstrance is probably about 1384.

To about the same time we may also ascribe the charming little poem *To Rosemounde*, seen by Dr. Furnivall at the Bodleian some years before, but first published by Professor Skeat in 1891. This is a ballade in three eight-line stanzas, with the refrain, "Thogh ye to me ne do no daliaunce". The poet asserts that he is as deep sunk in love as ever a cook smothered a fish in sauce, a simile from which we may very fairly gather that, however much he may have delighted to see the pretty Rosemounde dance, his love for her did not greatly disturb his peace of mind.

§ 57. **"The Parlement of Foules."**—The *Parlement of Foules* is one of Chaucer's earliest masterpieces. He had translated from French, Latin and Italian, and we can trace his progress by the increasing freedom with which he used his originals. In this poem also we find abundant traces of his reading. We have a summary of *Scipio's Dream* from Cicero; there are reminiscences of a few lines of Dante; there is a list of trees taken partly from the *Teseide*, partly from the *Roman de la Rose*; Chaucer takes also from the *Teseide* (Bk. vii. st. 51-66) no less than sixteen stanzas (ll. 183-294) describing the Garden of Love (some say already translated for *Palamon and Arcyte*), and he imitates from the *Planctus Naturae* of Alain de l'Isle (§ 25) his description of Nature and her birds, though he is wise enough to represent the birds as living creatures clustering round her instead of mere embroidery to her garment. He was writing a poem which needed ornament, and he took his ornament from where

[1] *rape*, hurry.

he could find it; but the spirit, the gaiety, humour, and
love of Nature are all his own, and regarded as a whole the
Parlement of Foules is as original as the *Midsummer
Night's Dream* or *As You Like It*.

The prelude to the poem opens with a tribute to the
"wonderful working of Love", of whom the writer professes to know nought save what he reads in books. For
pleasure or learning he reads oft, and lately spent a whole
day over Cicero's account of the dream of Scipio, and the
explanations of man's duty and destiny given by the
great Africanus:

> The wery hunter, slepynge in his bed,
> To wode agen his myndè goth anon;
> The jugè dremyth how his pleis been sped;
> The carter dremyth how his carte is gon;
> The riche of gold; the knyght fyght[1] with his fon[2];
> The syké[3] met[4] he drynkyth of the tonne;
> The lovere met he hath his lady wonne.

He had read *Scipio's Dream* before, but this time it set
him dreaming himself, and the great Africanus appeared
to lead him to a park "walled with grene stone", over
whose double gate were inscriptions in gold and black,
of invitation and of warning. This writing, he is told, is
for Love's servants, not for him—

> For thou of love hast lost thy taste, I gesse,
> As seek[5] man hath of swete and bitternesse.

He surveys the beautiful garden and the temple of Venus,
and comes at last to a lawn upon a hill where the Goddess
Nature is seated in leafy state, surrounded by birds of
every kind, for this is St. Valentine's Day, on which every
bird has to choose his mate. Six stanzas are filled with a
list of the birds, and then the poet comes to his story.
"Nature, the vicaire of the almighty lorde" (the phrase

[1] *fyght*, fighteth.   [2] *fon*, foes.   [3] *syke*, sick.
[4] *met*, dreams.   [5] *seek*, sick.

is from Alain de l'Isle), proclaims that every bird is now to make his choice: the tercel[1] eagles, who are "fowls royal", first; then the others after their degree. The first tercel makes suit, with many vows of true service, to the fair formel eagle whom Nature holds on her hand, and two other tercels pray likewise for her favour. Nature bids the other fowls pronounce which of the three is worthiest, and the goose, the turtle-dove, the cuckoo, speak on behalf of their several orders, amid many comments and interruptions. Nature bids the formel speak for herself, and having professed her loyalty she answers with a request for a respite till "this yeer be doon", and after that "to have her choice all free". The boon is granted; the other birds choose their mates; and with a roundel on the theme—

> Now welcom, somer, with thy sonné softe,
> That hast this wintrés weders over-shake,
> And driven awey the longé nightés blake—

the *Parlement* ends.

That this charming poem had an allegorical reference was long ago seen, and several wild guesses were made as to the marriage for which it was written before Dr. Koch showed that it was that of Richard II. and Anne of Bohemia. This solution and Dr. Koch's identification of one of the two rival eagles with Frederick Margrave of Meissen have been widely accepted, while Professor Emerson's suggestion of Prince Charles of France, the son of King Charles V., is generally preferred to Koch's backing of William of Bavaria (Baiern-Holland). In the *Life* of the Emperor Wenceslas we are told that the English ambassadors arrived at the court of Bohemia about January 1381 (they left London 26th December

---

[1] Among birds of prey the females were called *formels*, the males *tercels*, because they were supposed to be a third smaller. The derivation of *formel* is uncertain.

1380); and special mention is made of the fact that "the Princess Anne had already reached the age to choose herself a husband" (cf. ll. 626, 627). The marriage took place 14th January 1382, almost exactly when the year was "doon" (l. 647), and for the reasons already quoted from Dr. Koch (§ 38, 2) it seems certain that Chaucer was bidden to celebrate the courtship early in the following summer. Royal marriages were too likely to be broken off for poets to hymn them prematurely, and it is possible that the Queen, to whom Chaucer speaks of presenting his *Legende of Good Women*, and who took an immediate interest in English affairs, may herself have bidden him write this poem in her honour.

§ 58.[1] **"The Hous of Fame."**—The machinery of this poem involves the common mediæval fiction of a dream, which is said to have befallen the writer on 10th December in an unspecified year, probably 1380 (see § 38, 2). Chaucer's dream first takes him to a temple of glass dedicated to Venus, in which on a tablet he sees written the opening words of Virgil's *Aeneid*, followed by the whole story, which he gives in epitome in 317 lines. On leaving the temple he finds himself in a sandy plain, and sees a great golden eagle beginning to alight (end of Bk. i.). As he gazes at the eagle it seizes and bears him aloft, telling him not to be afraid, for it is sent from Jove, in compassion for the poet's dull and loveless life, to show him the Hous of Fame, where he shall find some game and desport. Where Fame dwells "thyn owne book it telleth", the eagle says, alluding to the description of the Palace of Fame in Ovid's *Metamorphoses*, xii. 33-63, on which Chaucer founds all the details of his own account. The eagle explains how the sounds of earth are borne aloft to Fame's House; and, as they fly through space, offers to

---

[1] I keep this section in its original place, after that dealing with the *Parlement*, rather than alter the section numbers.

teach him about the stars—an offer declined by the poet
on the ground that he is too old to learn. They reach
the hill on which the palace stands, and the eagle bids
Chaucer go in, while it awaits him outside (end of Bk. ii.).
Fame's House is built on a great rock of ice, inscribed
with names which melt away in the sun. The house itself
beggars description. The goddess sits on a throne of ruby
in a mighty hall set around with pillars on which stand
the great writers of past time. Suppliants approach, and
Fame sends for the wind-god Aeolus, who comes bearing
his golden and black trumps, the one of Fame, the other
of Slander. The various requests of other bands of suppliants are granted, refused, or reversed at the mere whim
of the goddess; and when a bystander asks Chaucer what
he is doing there, he answers that he seeks no fame for
himself, and is disappointed in his hope of gathering new
tidings. He hints, in fact, that though he is very interested
in seeing exactly how everything is done, he knew well
enough before he came both what men asked of the goddess and how she answered them. He leaves the hall, and
by the help of the eagle finds himself in a house sixty
miles long, filled with all the gossip of the world, represented in the likeness of its speakers—shipmen, pilgrims,
and pardoners being especially prominent. At the last he
sees a man who seems to be of great authority; and there
the poem breaks off. What we have of it consists altogether of 2158 lines, of which the first and second books
each occupy, roughly speaking, a quarter, and the last,
though unfinished, the remaining half. The poem was
probably written primarily for recitation at the Court,
and Dr. Brusendorff, in suggesting the connection of the
date of the dream on 10th December with the appointment two days later of an embassy to treat for the King's
marriage, has surmised also that the idea of it came to
Chaucer from a poem by Froissart, the *Temple d'Onneur*,

which ends with an obscure reference to a forthcoming marriage. Dr. Brusendorff thinks that only a single leaf of the original manuscript was lost, and that in the course of the sixty lines which this would contain the man of great authority was to make a veiled allusion to the forthcoming marriage of Richard and Anne. This seems a reasonable theory, and I apologise to Chaucer for having suggested, in earlier editions of this little book and elsewhere, that having been borne up to the *Hous of Fame* by the golden eagle he did not know how to get down again. I ought to have remembered that in dream-stories such difficulties are easily solved by the dreamer waking up. The dream-form may also excuse the length of the epitome of the *Aeneid* and other inequalities. It remains true, however, that the general plan of the poem is much less masterly than the workmanship of the sepaiate parts, in some of which the poet's individuality is exceptionally strongly marked. Indeed, in the conversation with the eagle, some lines from which have been quoted in § 20, he tells us more about himself than in any other poem.

The likeness of the *Hous of Fame* to Dante's *Divina Commedia* is not very apparent, yet it has been learnedly argued that this is the "som comedye" which, at the end of his *Troilus*, Chaucer prayed that God would send him might to make (see § 38, i.).[1] Both poems are in three books, both are visions, and in both the poet is conducted by a heaven-sent guide, who yet may not go everywhere with him. The idea of the golden eagle is taken from Dante (*Purgat.* ix.), so too is the specifying of the exact day of the vision. It is possible also that the part played by Virgil in the *Divina Commedia* suggested the epitome of the *Aeneid* already mentioned.

---

[1] If Dr. Brusendorff's dating is right it was written before *Troilus*, but in any case the influence of Dante's great work may be admitted, not only in a number of particular passages, but in its scheme.

In the *Hous of Fame* each book is preceded by an invocation, the second being suggested by the *Inferno*, ii. 7-9,
and the third by one in a similar position in Dante's
third book (*Parad.* i. 13-27). Minor imitations are too
numerous to be here quoted. But it is not only from
Dante that Chaucer borrowed. As he is upborne through
the clouds, he remarks:

> And tho thought I upon Boece,
> That wryteth, Thought may flee so hye,
> With fetheres of philosophye,
> To passen everych element;
> And whan he hath so fer y-went,
> Than may be seen, behynde his bak,
> Cloud and al that I of spak.

Chaucer's eagle is a much less formidable person than
the Philosophy of the *De Consolatione*, but there is a
philosophical side to his poem, and this is taken rather
from the early chapters of Boethius than from Dante,
whose seriousness was too deep for Chaucer's humour.

§ 57a. "Palamon and Arcyte" (The Knight's Tale).—
Mention has already been made (§ 51) of the theory of
Tyrwhitt, Ten Brink, and Skeat that this had previously
been written in stanzas; of the date 1381–82 assigned to
it by Professor Lowes and Emerson (§ 38, 2) on the
ground of allusions to a tempest and a parliament which,
if relevant at all, seem to me as likely to be reminiscences
as contemporary, and of my own belief that this story
in which Palamon is raised from misery to royalty and
happy marriage may be the "comedy" promised at the
end of *Troilus* (§ 38, 1). I find further evidence for placing
this story after the *Troilus* in the fact that Boccaccio's
description of the passage of Arcite's soul to the spheres,
omitted from its place in the Knight's Tale, is found in
Troilus, v. 1807-1827, apparently as an insertion (see the
note in the Globe text), which suggests that Chaucer in
rehandling the *Teseide* thought that this passage would

be more suitable to the already written *Troilus* and inserted it there. My own belief that this gives us the true
order is based mainly on the unstinted freedom with
which Chaucer in his interest in *Troilus and Criseyde* had
allowed himself to tell their story compared with his
watchful eye as to length in the Knight's Tale. Here
he reduces the 9054 lines of the *Teseide* to 2250, despite
the space given to descriptions of lists and temples and
moralisings from Boece. It seems to me that the brevity
is a conscious reaction from the length of *Troilus*, and
now and again Chaucer pats himself on the back for it.
The brevity makes him all the more dramatic in his treat-
ment of the two cousins who quarrel in prison as to which
shall be the lover of the princess they see walking in the
garden below them; who meet again in the green wood
and fight for her, and are allowed at last by Theseus to
decide their claims at a great tournament, the result of
which is overruled by Arcyte's death. Chaucer did not
put his heart into this as into *Troilus*, but it is a glittering
triumph of his art.

§ 59. **"The Legende of Good Women."**—The *Legende
of Good Women*, as Chaucer planned it, was intended to
consist of a prologue, the stories of nineteen women who
have been true to love, and lastly the praise of the crown
of womanhood, Queen Alcestis, who gave up her own life
to save her husband's. Such a series of poems had plainly
been for some time in Chaucer's mind. The goodness of
Alceste is the subject of two stanzas in the *Troilus*; and
in the *Hous of Fame* (Bk. i. ll. 388-426), after telling the
story of Dido out of Virgil's *Aeneid*, he had given a list
of other faithful women, to whom, doubtless, he meant to
apply the phrase he uses of Dido, that if it were not too
long to endite he would have liked to have written her
love in full. The actual impulse to write the poem and
give it the queen "at Eltham or at Sheene" (royal palaces)

Ten Brink and Skeat connected with the leave given to Chaucer on 17th February 1385 to appoint a permanent deputy to his comptrollership, regarding it as a mark of gratitude for this particular favour. We now know that the privilege was not openly obtained for Chaucer by the Queen, yet the date, 1385, which Skeat suggested, cannot be far wrong, though to give time for all the other poems Chaucer began after 1380 it is safer to assign it to the following year, 1386. Lydgate in the Prologue to his *Fall of Princes* (see § 35) says that the *Legende* was written "at the request of the quene", and though this may only be an inference stated as a fact, it is quite likely to be true.

We have already had to quote for other purposes two passages which strike the keynote of the prologue. Chaucer tells us of his reverence for the authority of books, and how only his love of flowers in May, and especial worship of the daisy, can tear him from them (§ 20). One May Day he goes to sleep in a leafy bower, and dreams that Love threatens him for his heresies, that he is forgiven on the intercession of Love's Queen, Alcestis (§ 37), who bids him write "a glorious legende of goode women" as an easy penance. "Legende", it must be explained, is here used in its ecclesiastical sense of a lectionary, and Chaucer was bidden to write twenty lessons on the women faithful in love who were Cupid's saints, to rival the lessons on the lives of the saints of the Church in the breviary. The legends actually written are nine in number, celebrating (1) Cleopatra, who is represented (not quite in accordance, as Chaucer imagines, with "storial sooth") as a martyr to her love for Antony; (2) Thisbe, who refused to survive her lover Pyramus (see Bottom's play in the *Midsummer Night's Dream*); (3) Dido; (4) the two victims of Jason's treachery, Hypsipyle and Medea; (5) Lucretia; (6) Ariadne; (7) Philomela, the victim of Tereus; (8) Phyllis, who slew herself

for love of Demophon; (9) Hypermnestra, who accepted
death at her father's hands rather than treacherously kill
her husband. By the aid of some hints in the Prologue, and
of a curious mention of these "seintes legendes of Cupide"
in the talk which precedes the Man of Law's story in the
Canterbury Tales, Dr. Skeat made a fair guess as to the
names of the other ten women, in addition to Alcestis,
whose praises Chaucer was too tired to hymn. For the
nine stories he finished, Chaucer had recourse chiefly to
the *Metamorphoses* and *Heroides* of Ovid, but he used
also two Latin works by Boccaccio, viz. his *De Claris
Mulieribus* and *De Genealogia Deorum*, while the story
of Dido is taken mainly from Virgil, and that of Hypsipyle
and Medea from the *Historia Trojana* of Guido delle
Colonne. Of the Prologue two versions are extant: one
preserved only in a single manuscript and long thought
to be an early draft was proved by Dr. Livingston Lowes
in 1904 to be a revised version almost certainly written
after Queen Anne's death, 7th June 1394, since, in accordance with the King's passionate grief, which would veto
mention of her, the lines bidding Chaucer take the book
to her are omitted. It seems so strange that he should have
returned to this task in 1394 when he had his *Canterbury
Tales* still on hand, that we could almost believe that he
had kept in touch with the "legende" by writing one
of the poems "yere by yere" (see l. 481). In the revision
Chaucer shortened the 545 lines of the first version to 511,
though introducing a long passage on love-tales and a
reference to his own library of sixty books of them.

The great charm of the *Legende of Good Women* consists in these delightful prologues, with their chat about
Chaucer's fondness for books and worship of the daisy,
and the scene in the Garden of Love, in which Alcestis
intercedes for him. Of the separate legends many are as
well told as we can imagine possible, notably those of

Thisbe, Dido, and Ariadne. But here, as in the tragedies of the Monk's Tale, Chaucer, partly under the inspiration of Boccaccio, embarked upon a task against which his judgment rebelled before he was half-way through with it. To write twenty stories in succession on as many variations of a single theme was to court monotony, and the monotony wearies the poet perhaps before most of his readers have become aware of it.

§ 60. **Review of Chaucer's Second Period.**—In reviewing at the end of the last chapter Chaucer's progress up to the date of his second Italian journey (1378–79), we noted that during the ten or twelve years which may separate his earliest poem from the *Compleynt of Mars* we could only attribute to him the composition of about one-seventh part of his extant poetry, even though the whole of the Man of Law's Tale and part of that of the Monk were rather violently detached from their place in the *Canterbury Tales* to swell the work of these years. The period we have now been surveying is only about half as long, but was nearly three times as productive.[1] Possibly the more serious study of Italian models during and after his second visit to Italy gave Chaucer this new poetic impulse; possibly it was due to an increased interest in literature taken by Richard II. as he grew to manhood, or to the literary influence of Anne of Bohemia. We have noted how both the *Parlement of Foules* and the *Legende of Good Women* were connected with the Queen; and Richard II., who could give an enormous sum for two volumes of French romances, and who took an interest in the work of the "moral" Gower, may also have spurred Chaucer on to write. We know that the poet's life was no longer perpetually broken into by his despatch on foreign

---

[1] According to my addition the exact number of lines is 14,337 as against 5313, but such measuring of poetry by the yard is rather incongruous.

missions: the references in the *Hous of Fame* and the *Legende* to his books and his reading show us that, however irksome his work at the Custom House may have been, it left him free to devote his evenings to study and composition, with notable results. It may, indeed, be said that all Chaucer's poetry during this period bears the trace of hard work. He is no longer content, as in the *Lyf of Seint Cecyle* and *Grisilde,* to translate his author as he may; he alters and improves with a free hand, and brings all his learning to the embellishment of particular passages. The *Parlement* and the *Hous of Fame* especially illustrate this building up of poems, which yet remain essentially original, by the help of jewels sought for wherever they could be found. But if Chaucer read diligently during these years, his increased consciousness of what belonged to his art in no way checked the growth of his own poetic individuality. The increase of ease is very marked. He is on better terms with himself and his readers, and chats about himself and his own tastes with good confidence that people will be interested. In such chats, and in the character of Sir Pandarus, we see the development of his humour, and we feel that this humour is the outcome of an increased knowledge of life. Already he is groping vaguely for a subject which shall give free scope to his now perfected powers; and soon on the King's high road to Canterbury he finds the materials which gave all his genius full room to play.

CHAPTER VI

THE CANTERBURY TALES

§ 61. **Did Chaucer go on Pilgrimage himself?**—On the last day of their journey from Southwark to Canterbury, when his pilgrims are already approaching their destination, and all save one of them are supposed to have told their tales, Chaucer stops to note the exact position of the sun as they rode into a village, and to tell us that from this and the length of his shadow, nearly twice his own height, he guessed the time as about four in the afternoon. He goes on to say that "the moones exaltacioun, I mene *Libra*, alwey gan ascende", making for once a blunder in his astrology, for the moon's exaltation is *Taurus*, not *Libra*. An attempt has been made to amend this, by reading "In mena" for "I mene", with an interpretation that the moon was rising at four o'clock in the middle of *Libra*, which, about the time Chaucer was writing, could only happen on 20th April in the one year 1385. We now know, however, that in 1385 Chaucer received his pension personally on 24th April, and he could hardly have got back in time to do this. We must thus abandon this interpretation and only remark that Chaucer's way of noting the hour, though it seems strange to people used to reckoning time only by their watches, is not the calculation of a student over his books. It suggests that he made his guess in the open air, and noted the moon rising so early in the afternoon with his own eyes. It suggests, that is, like two or three other little touches, that the poet one spring rode along the highway and made the pilgrimage to Canterbury in his own person. There is no sound reason to be alleged against this, and there will be no harm if we proceed to agree with Dr. Skeat that the best day for a large company to start on a four days' pilgrimage from Southwark to Canterbury would have been a Wednesday, and that since 18th April fell on a Wednesday in 1387 this may have been the year in which Chaucer himself was a pilgrim. We must not, however, go further than this, and imagine that the pilgrims whom he describes in the Prologue were suggested to him by those with whom he may have ridden.   For (1) his pilgrims range over too large a proportion of mediaeval life to have been based on a haphazard company; (2) some of them may have been described to fit in with stories already written and planned to be assigned to them; and (3) evidence is being collected that several were described, with satirical touches, to suggest real persons of Chaucer's day, for the amusement of his friends. Some details of this evidence, which is being collected by or under the inspiration of Prof. J. M. Manly (see his *New Light on Chaucer*, 1926), will be found in § 87, but the work is still (1930) in progress.

§ 62. **The Idea of the Canterbury Tales.**— Whether we accept the view that Chaucer himself went on a pilgrimage to Canterbury one fine April, or content ourselves with remembering that at least from October 1385 when he was appointed a Justice of the Peace for Kent he must often have seen companies of pilgrims on the road, there would seem no need to send him far afield for the idea of his famous *Tales*. For many years, however, it was assumed that Chaucer must have been guided to his happiest inspiration by the example of the *Decamerone* of his contemporary, Boccaccio. In the *Decamerone* seven fine ladies and three fine gentlemen take refuge from the great plague of Florence (A.D. 1348) in a beautiful garden, and there during ten days of forgetfulness of the misery from which they have fled, each tells ten stories, mostly of amorous adventure, until the century of tales is duly complete. The contrast of this scheme with that of Chaucer's holds good whether the latter was consciously improving on an Italian model or ignorant of its existence and merely taking a step forward from the point he had already reached in his *Legende of Good Women*. It is certainly improbable that he possessed a copy of the *Decamerone* himself. A few of his stories cover the same ground as some of Boccaccio's, but we know that he took

Grisilde from Petrarch's version, not from the *Deca-merone*, and in the other instances Latin or French parallels have been found which are mostly closer to Chaucer than anything in Boccaccio. Had the English poet possessed a copy of such a treasury of stories he would almost certainly have used at least a few of them, and as he has not done this we must conclude that he either did not know the *Decamerone* at all, or knew it only by hearsay, or by a casual glance during one of his Italian journeys. On the whole, then, we shall be quite safe in allowing Chaucer to retain the entire credit for the framework of the great series of *Tales* with which his name has always been chiefly connected.

§ 63. **The Two Sides of Pilgrimages.**—While the horror inspired by the murder of Becket was still fresh, the pilgrims to the scene of his martyrdom were doubtless inspired by a feeling of pure devotion. It was in such a spirit that Louis VII. of France came to return thanks for the recovery of his son from a dangerous illness, and offered at the tomb a ruby worth a king's ransom; and again, that our own Richard I., on his release from captivity, as soon as he landed at Sandwich, walked on foot to Canterbury Cathedral. In 1220 the saint's body had been translated to the gorgeous shrine prepared for its reception, and perhaps this great ceremony, the cost of which burdened the finances of five Archbishops, marked a new epoch in the devotion to St. Thomas. His shrine became one of the sights of Europe; the precincts of the cathedral were filled with booths as for a perpetual fair, and a pilgrimage in his honour was soon a pleasant holiday, in which the devotional element depended entirely on the character of the pilgrim. In 1370, on the fourth jubilee of Becket's martyrdom, Simon of Sudbury, at that time Bishop of London, as he met the great crowd of pilgrims on the road, told them outright that their pilgrimage would avail them nothing. A few years later Wyclif and his followers condemned the levity and superstition of the pilgrims still more severely. But the popularity of the shrine remained as yet undiminished. The crowd returned the reproaches of the Bishop with threats and curses, and when, eleven years later, he was murdered by the London mob, his death was regarded as a judgment for his sacrilegious speech. So the merry pilgrimages went on, and pipers and story-tellers found their profit in amusing the holiday-makers by the way. But at times throughout the journey, and at the sight of the sacred relics of the saint, the old devotional feeling would break out afresh. In every company, we may be sure, there were a few simple-hearted men and women whose religious enthusiasm at such times would be contagious, though it could not check the merriment and ribaldry with which the journey was enlivened. If a pilgrimage was a holiday, it was still a holiday sanctioned by religion, of which every man could make the use he chose.

§ 64. **Chaucer's Pilgrims at the Tabard.**—The Tabard Inn, at which Chaucer represents his pilgrims as assembling, was part of the London estate of the Abbots of Hyde, and lay in the High Street of Southwark, a little to the south of London Bridge, and consequently not far from the Chapel of St. Thomas, which was built on one of its piers. It was called the Tabard from its sign of a sleeveless coat, now the traditional dress of a herald, and was probably about 1385 the chief among the many inns in Southwark. To travel in company was advisable, not only for merriment, but for safety against robbers; and as wayfarers in the fourteenth century started with the sun, the intending pilgrims, and Chaucer among them, made their way to the inn overnight. When the last had arrived, there were "wel nine and twenty" of them, a

number which tallies with the list of the pilgrims only if
two of the "preestes thre" with the Prioress indicate the
Monk and Friar whose descriptions follow hers. Mediaeval
pilgrims were drawn from all classes; and all classes from
a knight to a poor ploughman and a begging friar were
here represented. The KNIGHT, a veteran soldier of the
Cross, was just returned from a voyage, and brought
with him his son, a young SQUIRE, ripe for love-making
or fighting, and a YEOMAN. Not less than nine of the
pilgrims were in the service of the Church. Of these,
the chief was a courtly and tender-hearted PRIORESS,
escorted by her "CHAPELEYN", or secretary (as the SECOND
NUN), and three PRIESTS, or more probably only one.
Next to the Prioress is ranked a MONK, "a manly man,
to been an abbot able", fonder of hunting than of books,
and from the description of his horses, greyhounds, and
dress, a person of some importance. A FRIAR, who found
his glib tongue very useful in begging; a SOMPNOUR,
or summoner of offenders against ecclesiastical law; a
PARDONER, who sold pardons, and exhibited imaginary
relics to be kissed for a groat—these represented the
lowest elements in the Church, of which the Prioress
and Monk were respectable, if rather worldly, members.
Ample atonement is made, however, in the portrait of the
poor PARSON, in whom Chaucer depicts an ideal parish
priest. With him we must reckon the CLERK OF OXFORD,
who "had not getten him yet a benefice", but was doubtless in orders. He was as devoted to learning, and helping
others to learn, as the Parson to the care of his parish;
and the two, in their simple-minded devotion, represent
all that was best in the Church. From the other learned
professions there came a SERGEANT-AT-LAW and a DOC-
TOR OF MEDICINE, both clever men: the Man of Law, a
busy man enough, but pretending to be busier still by
way of advertisement; the Doctor something of a miser.

A FRANKLIN, or country gentleman, very fond of good eating and drinking, is the person of highest rank among the remaining pilgrims, who comprise a MERCHANT; a SHIPMAN, not much better than a pirate; a MILLER, skilled in taking thrice his proper tolls; a rascal COOK; a MANCIPLE (or purchaser of provisions for one of the Inns of Court) and a REEVE (or farm-bailiff), both of them able to hoodwink their employers; and, as against all these rogues, five respectable London Burgesses (a HABERDASHER, CARPENTER, WEAVER, DYER, and TAPYCER, or tapestry-maker), all of one guild; and a poor PLOUGHMAN, brother to the Parson, and his counterpart for goodness. Besides the Prioress and her Nun, there was one other woman among the pilgrims, a WIFE OF BATH, expert in cloth-making and in getting the better of husbands, of whom she had had five.

The Host of the Tabard, Harry Bailey, a great fellow with bright eyes, fit to be a marshal in a hall, was so pleased with this varied company of guests that when they had supped he proposed to them "a mirth", to which they good-humouredly assented before they knew what it was. The Host's plan for their amusement was that each pilgrim should tell two stories on the way to Canterbury and two on their return, the best story to be rewarded by a supper at the common cost. He himself would ride with them as guide and judge. The plan was accepted; the pilgrims went to their beds, and the next morning were roused by the Host, who duly started the story-telling as soon as they reached "the wateryng of Seint Thomas", the second milestone on the old road to Canterbury.

§ 65. **Number of the Tales.**—According to Harry Bailey's proposal, each of the twenty-nine pilgrims was to tell four stories, so that if his scheme had been carried out in full the number of the *Canterbury Tales* would have been 116, besides a supplementary one told by a Canon's Yeoman who joins them on the road. Including this supplementary story the number actually written is twenty-four, of which one (the Squire's) is left half told, and another (the Cook's) scarcely begun, while the poet himself is allowed two attempts. The pilgrims who are left altogether silent are the Knight's Yeoman, the Plough-man, and the five Burgesses. The five Burgesses are not described individually but as a group, so that we find we have the part or whole of a story told by all save two of the characters in whom we are specially interested, and for one of these, the Yeoman, Chaucer had ready the old tale of *Gamelyn* to rewrite. Thus, if his scheme had forecast only one tale from each pilgrim, we should not have to regard it as left very incomplete. The needless magnitude of his plan is perhaps the only argument in favour of the view that it was intended to imitate the hundred stories of the *Decamerone*.

§ 66. **Order in which the Tales were told.**—We have already alluded more than once to the chats on the road by which the Tales were intended to be linked together and the monotony of story-telling relieved. Prologues of some kind are attached to all of the Tales that have come down to us, but only about half of them are real links, giving the verdict of the company on the last tale, as well as the invitation of the Host to another of the pilgrims to tell a new one. By the help of these real links we are able to group together in three instances two, in one three, in one four, and in one seven, or really eight, of the Tales. Moreover, in these prologues and links we have:

(i.) References to six places on the road, viz. Dept-ford, Greenwich, Rochester, Sittingbourne, Boughton-under-Blee, and a rather mysterious village called Bob-up-and-Down.

(ii.) Remarks by both the Clerk and the Merchant,

implying that the Wife of Bath's Tale had been told before theirs, and presumably on the same day.

(iii.) Four distinct notes of time, viz. prime[1]; ten in the forenoon, on 18th April; prime, again; and four in the afternoon; besides other less precise references.

Now the order of the *Tales* differs considerably in the different manuscripts which have come down to us, but in the best manuscript of all (called the Ellesmere, from the family to whom it belonged) it is as follows—the letters, arrows, and other annotations being, of course, inserted for our own ends:

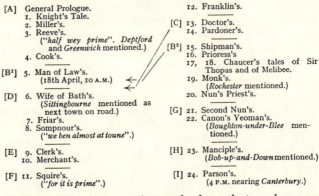

[A] General Prologue.
  1. Knight's Tale.
  2. Miller's.
  3. Reeve's.
    ("*half wey prime*". *Deptford* and *Greenwich* mentioned.)
  4. Cook's.

[B¹] 5. Man of Law's.
    (18th April, 10 A.M.)

[D] 6. Wife of Bath's.
    (*Sittingbourne* mentioned as next town on road.)
  7. Friar's.
  8. Sompnour's.
    ("*we ben almost at toune*".)

[E] 9. Clerk's.
  10. Merchant's.

[F] 11. Squire's.
    ("*for it is prime*".)

12. Franklin's.

[C] 13. Doctor's.
  14. Pardoner's.

[B²] 15. Shipman's.
  16. Prioress's
  17, 18. Chaucer's tales of Sir Thopas and of Melibee.
  19. Monk's.
    (*Rochester* mentioned.)
  20. Nun's Priest's.

[G] 21. Second Nun's.
  22. Canon's Yeoman's.
    (*Boughton-under-Blee* mentioned.)

[H] 23. Manciple's.
    (*Bob-up-and-Down* mentioned.)

[I] 24. Parson's.
    (4 P.M. nearing *Canterbury*.)

The nine lines drawn at intervals show that we have no links to connect the tales which they separate. There is, indeed, such a link between the Manciple's and the Parson's, but as the Manciple's is apparently told in the morning and the Parson's at four in the afternoon, the probability that there is some mistake prevents us from regarding these two tales as really joined together.

---

[1] The meaning of this word varies. Chaucer seems to use it for 6 A.M. and also for the hours between 6 and 9 A.M.

The order of the *Tales* as thus given by the Ellesmere MS. seems very nearly right, but there is one obvious error in it. In the Prologue to the Wife of Bath's Tale, the pilgrims are not far from Sittingbourne. In the Prologue to the Monk's, the Host says: "Lo, Rowchestre stant heeré fasté by", and as Rochester comes before Sittingbourne on the Canterbury road, we see at once that we must move the group of tales (15-20) which includes the Monk's to come before that (6-8) which includes the Wife of Bath's. We are confirmed in doing this by finding that the Shipman's Prologue (which heads the Monk's section) is actually placed after the Man of Law's Tale in probably the oldest MS. now extant, and that it fits in exactly as a link between the two tales. In this MS. (Harl. 7334) the link is ascribed to the Squire, to whom it is quite unsuited, and in others to the Sompnour, but in one manuscript (Arch. Seld. B. 14) it is duly credited to the Shipman, and we are not without means of guessing how the confusion arose. A passage in the tale shows clearly that it was originally written to be told by a married woman, *i.e.* by the Wife of Bath, the only married woman among the pilgrims, and while this was her story, she was probably intended to follow the Man of Law in amusing the company on the second day. When a new prologue and tale were written for the Wife, these should have been assigned to the third day, but the scribes confused the positions of her new tale and her old, and then, not knowing what to do with the Shipman's Prologue, gave it, some to the Squire, others to the Sompnour, merely because their names also began with S.

Together with the Shipman's group Dr. Furnivall (to whom, in combination with Henry Bradshaw, the corrected ordering of the *Canterbury Tales* is entirely due) moved up, in reverse order, the linked tales of the Doctor

and Pardoner, *i.e.* whereas these tales in the Ellesmere
MS. precede the Shipman's group, he brought them up
after the Shipman's group and before the Wife of Bath's.
This change spreads the extant tales fairly equally over
the four days, but is not supported by anything in the
text or the arrangement of any extant manuscript, and
has led to two discordant notations for the groups, that
of the Chaucer Society by the letters A-I and Professor
Manly's by the numerals i-ix. The lettering of the different groups, A, B, C, etc., is the one generally adopted in
all references to the *Tales*.

§ 67. **Stages and Duration of the Pilgrimage.**—The time
occupied by the journey to Canterbury was probably no
less than four days. This may seem very excessive for a
ride of only fifty-six miles; but we must remember that
many of the pilgrims were ill-mounted and inexpert
riders (thus of the Shipman it is said "he rode upon a
rouncy as he coude") and that even main-roads in the
fourteenth century were often little better than quag-
mires, and this Canterbury road in particular is twice
spoken of by the Host as "the slough". Travellers on
urgent business, no doubt, rode considerable distances,
as much as forty miles in a day; but from twenty to
twenty-five miles seems to have been considered a good
day's journey. For a mixed company of holiday-makers
forty-six miles in three days over fairly level roads, and
ten miles for the last day's ride over Blean Hill, would
not apparently have been abnormally slow progress.
Moreover, we have two important precedents to guide us.
In 1358 the Queen-mother Isabella went on a pilgrimage
to Canterbury. She left London on 7th June, slept that
night at Dartford, slept at Rochester on 8th June, at
Ospringe on 9th June, and reached Canterbury on the
10th, *i.e.* on the fourth day from starting. In 1360 John
of France in his journey from London to Calais slept

at Dartford 1st July, dined there next day, slept at Rochester 2nd July, dined at Sittingbourne and slept at Ospringe 3rd July, reaching Canterbury 4th July. The records of other fourteenth-century pilgrimages confirm the presumption that Dartford, Rochester, and Ospringe (where some trace of the old Pilgrims' House still exists) were the regular sleeping-places on the road; and if we imagine our pilgrims as having kept to them, we shall get the simplest explanation of all the references to places and time in the conversations, and have the journey divided into fairly equal lengths. The two references to "prime" dispel the old idea that the whole pilgrimage was accomplished on a single day. If we endeavour to compress it into two days, we must make the pilgrims ride the almost impossible distance of forty-six miles to Ospringe on the first day, and only ten on the second. If we allow three days, we must still make the pilgrims ride thirty miles—more than half the distance—on the first day, sixteen on the second, and ten on the third. We must also make the words of the Host to the Man of Law, which have all the appearance of beginning a day's story-telling after a late start, merely mark a resumption of it after an early dinner. The four days' journey is exposed to no such difficulties or inequalities, and is therefore adopted in the following summary of the incidents of the journey. It must be noted that the 17th April 1385 (old style) would answer to the 25th April of the reformed calendar.

§ 68. **Tales of the First Day.**—For the first mile or more of their journey the drone of the Miller's bagpipes provided the pilgrims with sufficient entertainment; but at the second milestone, "the wateryng of Seint Thomas", the Host called his company together to draw lots as to who should tell the first tale. "By aventure, or sort, or cas", or rather by a little arrangement on the Host's part, the shortest "cut" fell to the Knight, the person of greatest dignity among the pilgrims; and with a good grace he forthwith told his story of the love of Palamon and Arcyte for the fair Emelye, the "yongė suster shene" of the great Theseus, "duke" of Athens. Young and old praised the Knight's tale as a noble story, and the Host in high delight called on the Monk to cap it with another. But the Miller, who had had time to quench the thirst caused by his piping, and was now sadly drunk, insisted on being allowed to tell what he called a "noble tale", about a carpenter and his wife and a young Oxford clerk. The carpenter is shamelessly befooled in the story; and the Reeve, who had been bred a carpenter himself, retaliated with a tale of the revenge taken by two young Cambridge clerks on a miller who had succeeded in stealing the college corn despite all their precautions. When the Reeve was on the point of beginning his tale Deptford and Greenwich were both in sight, and the time was "half wey prime", *i.e.* between 7 and 8 A.M. His story was succeeded by that of the Cook, of which we have only the first sixty lines, introducing to us Perkin Revelour, an idle London apprentice. By the help of Reeve and Cook, Deptford must have been reached about nine o'clock, and the pilgrims no doubt stopped here for an early dinner. When they remounted their horses the Yeoman may have been the first speaker. In many of the manuscripts the *Tale of Gamelyn* is here inserted—a poem or "lay" in rough, vigorous verse, probably at least a quarter of a century earlier than the *Canterbury Tales*. The plot is similar to that of Shakespeare's *As You Like It*, and Chaucer no doubt intended to retell it as a woodland tale exactly suited to the sturdy Yeoman. No other stories, or raw materials for stories, belonging to this day have come down to us, and we can only guess that the five Burgesses were the narrators for the rest of the afternoon, until at about five or six o'clock the pilgrims finished their first day's ride of fifteen miles, and rested at Dartford for supper and a night's lodging.

§ 69. **Tales of the Second Day.**—Between Dartford and Rochester lay no town of any size, and, like King John of France before them, the pilgrims were therefore obliged to dine where they had slept, and did not start until nearly ten o'clock. The Host noted the hour by the length of his shadow (incidentally letting us know that the day was 18th April), and with a little exhortation against wasting time, called on the Man of Law for a tale. He has no thrifty tale to tell, is the reply, for Chaucer has told them all.

> But nathèlees, I recchè noght a bene
> Though I come after hym, with hawè-bakè
> I speke in prose and lat hym rymès makè.

He remembers a tale once told him by a merchant, and after these apologies we have given us the beautiful story of Constance (see § 47). "This *was* a thrifty tale for the nones", is the Host's comment, and he calls on the Parson, as another "learned man of lore", to be the next speaker. Unfortunately in his enthusiasm he raps out an oath, for which the good Parson reproves him, thereby provoking the wrath of the Shipman against his Lollardy. The Shipman tells a story himself of how an unsuspicious merchant was deceived by his wife and a friar; and then the Host, always anxious to give the gentle-folk due precedence, courteously asks the Prioress to tell her tale. After a beautiful invocation, she recites the history of a little chorister murdered by the Jews for his devotion to the Blessed Virgin, telling the legend so perfectly as to hush even the most boisterous of the pilgrims. The silence was broken by the Host calling Chaucer to him with a joke on his stoutness and abstracted look. The poet's contribution is the inimitable *Tale of Sir Thopas*, a parody on the long-winded romances then going out of fashion; and the

Host, who could only see the absurdity and not the fun, soon bade him stop and "tell something in prose". The *Tale of Melibee*, an allegory of prudence, was Chaucer's second attempt, and this was heard out to the bitter end. The next story-teller, however, the Monk, endured the poet's first fate, for his string of tragedies, as we have seen (§ 48), was interrupted when he had told but seventeen of them. The Nun's Priest, who followed him, was far more successful. Indeed, his story of the gallant Cock who fell a victim to Reynard the Fox, and escaped from between his teeth by his own wit, is one of the very best of all the tales. It probably closed the story-telling for the day, as Rochester had been spoken of as "fastè by" ere the Monk began his tragedies, and it was at Rochester that the pilgrims must have slept their second night.

§ 70. **Tales of the Third Day.**—We have no conversation on the road to tell us how the third day's story-telling began, but according to Dr. Furnivall's conjecture, the Doctor's tale of Appius and Virginia, and the Pardoner's of Death and the Three Brothers, came early on this morning. The Pardoner wanted both a drink and a bite of a cake before he began, and after prefacing his tale with a sufficiently candid account of his method of earning a living, wound up by handing round his relics to be kissed, much to the Host's indignation. The Wife of Bath imitated the Pardoner in the frankness of her history of her married life, and told a story of the Court of Arthur, illustrating the fondness of women for getting their own way. While listening to her matrimonial experiences, the Friar and Sompnour had nearly come to blows; and as the pilgrims were approaching Sittingbourne, each told a tale to the discredit of the other's profession. After dining at Sittingbourne, the Host called on the Clerk to tell "som murie thyng of aventures", and was rewarded with the beautiful tale of the patience of

Grisilde. This, or rather the *envoy* which Chaucer rather incongruously added to it, inspired the Merchant to narrate the trickery and hardihood of an unfaithful wife, relieving the sordid story of January and May with some pleasant fairy humours. By the time his story was ended, the pilgrims must have ridden the six miles from Sittingbourne to Ospringe, and alighted there to pass the night at the old Pilgrims' House.

§ 71. **Tales of the Fourth Day.**—The next morning the Squire opened the story-telling with his half-told tale of Cambuscan, the Magic Horse, and the tender-hearted Princess who could understand all the language of birds. This was followed by the Franklin's story of a woman's loyalty to her word, and by the Second Nun's *Legend of Seint Cecyle*. As this last was finished, and the pilgrims, five miles on their road, had arrived at Boughton-under-Blee, a Canon and his Yeoman overtook them. The Canon was an alchemist who, in trying to turn lead into gold, had ruined both himself and his dupes. His servant's free talk drove him from the company, and the Yeoman then told a story of another Canon who robbed a poor priest by his pretended discoveries. The pilgrims were now toiling up Blean Hill, and the Cook, who was heavy with sleep or drink, had fallen so far behind that the Host feared for his safety. A quarrel between the Cook and the Manciple having been patched up, the latter tells a story as to how crows became black. At last all the pilgrims save the Parson are supposed to have told their tales, and the Host for the second time calls on the good man to keep his troth. He is a southern man, he says, and "kan nat geeste *rum, ram, ruf* by lettre", like the northern alliterative poets, but he will "telle a murie tale in prose". This proves to be a sermon on penitence, and to a discourse on the text: "Stondeth upon the weyes, and seeth, and axeth of olde pathes, which is the goode weye, and

walketh in that wey, and ye shal fynde refresshynge for
your soules", the merry company, at last reminded of the
object of its pilgrimage, draws near the city which en-
shrined the bones of the great Archbishop. Chaucer, alas,
does not even tell us of the entry into Canterbury, but
in the *Tale of Beryn*, an unknown continuator has pic-
tured the pilgrims at the Chequers of the Hope Inn, and
told us, in his own fashion, of what befell on their visit to
the shrine. In his *Tale of Thebes*, Lydgate essays to tell
the first story on the return journey. But neither of these
well-meaning admirers of Chaucer can supply their
master's place.

§ 72. **The Prologue.**—The number of words now
obsolete in the Prologue to the *Canterbury Tales* is unusually high, and for this reason it should not be read the
first among Chaucer's poems; nevertheless it usually is
read first, and is so well known that little need here be
said of it. For keen observation and vivid presentment
this gallery of character-sketches has never been surpassed. The portraits, we should note, seem all such as one
traveller might draw of another. There is no attempt to
show that the best of the pilgrims had their weak points,
and the worst their good ones. For the best Chaucer has
hearty admiration, for the worst a boundless tolerance,
which yet only thinly cloaks the keenest satire. One and
all he views from his holiday standpoint, building up his
descriptions with such notes as he would naturally gather
as he rode along with them on his pilgrimage—notes of
dress, of speech and manner, of their talk about themselves and their doings—until we can see his fellow-
pilgrims as clearly as if we, too, had mounted our rouncies
and ridden along with them. It would be pleasant to chat
about each of the pilgrims in turn: to wonder why the
Knight had never fought in the war with France, or to
note that hints for the character of the Prioress are taken

from the *Roman de la Rose*, and that the emphasis laid
on her manners and deportment is probably due to the
fact that her Priory, like that of St. Mary's, Winchester,
described in the Chaucer Society's *Essays*, may have been
a finishing school for girls and a residence for gentle ladies.
But for such details students must be referred to annotated editions of the Prologue, or to some of the numerous
books which have been written round about Chaucer and
the *Canterbury Tales*.

   § 73. **Tales of the Gentles.**— (i.) The KNIGHT'S Tale is
founded on the *Teseide* of Boccaccio. The *Teseide* contains 9054 lines, the Knight's Tale 2050, of which only
about 270 are translated from the Italian and another
500 adapted, so that Chaucer left himself free play. He
differs from Boccaccio in making Palamon see Emily
first, in making the cousins quarrel over their love, and
in representing Emily as ignorant of it. As already noted,
it has been conjectured that this tale is a recast of an
earlier poem, in seven-line stanzas, containing "al the
love of Palamon and Arcyte", which is thought to have
followed the *Teseide* much more closely. It is much more
likely, however, that Chaucer made preliminary use of
the *Teseide* in earlier poems in stanzas and then wrote
the story as a whole substantially in its present form, than
that he made a complete earlier version and used bits of
this in other poems. The Knight's is the longest of the
Canterbury Tales, and the most splendid and ornate. The
descriptions of the three temples of Mars, Venus, and
Diana are the most famous of all the "purple patches"
in Chaucer. The entry of Theseus into Athens, the two
cousins catching their first sight of Emily from their prison
window, the sudden meeting in the woods, the fight and
its interruption by Theseus and his hunting-party, the
mustering for the tourney, the death of Arcyte—these
form a succession of pictures of singular vividness and

colour. The characters of Palamon, the single-hearted lover, and Arcyte, torn between love and honour, are slightly sketched. Theseus, the older knight, chivalrous in defence of women, hot-tempered and cruel to his enemies, yet easily pacified and ready to laugh at the absurdities of lovers, is a much more finished portrait. As a story-teller the SQUIRE is worthy of his father. His tale is conceived in the same chivalrous vein, but is founded on some Eastern original not yet identified. The great Cambuscan may be traced ultimately to the travels of Marco Polo; the Horse of Brass and the Magic Ring, Mirror, and Sword are part of the common machinery of Eastern tales. The "falcon peregryn", to whom Canacee is so pitiful, is doubtless an injured princess metamorphosed by some magician. But the tale remains "half told", and even Spenser, in his *Faerie Queene*, has not been able to satisfy our curiosity as to how it should end. We may be sure that Chaucer's use of his unknown originals in this poem was extremely free, and the amusing passage in which the people comment on the miraculous gifts is characteristically his own.

(ii.) The Tales of the CLERK, MAN OF LAW, and FRANKLIN are linked together by their common exaltation of a single virtue to the exclusion of the rest. The Clerk magnifies Patience, the Lawyer (on whom the tale was foisted when he had announced his intention to speak in prose) Fortitude, the Franklin, Truth. The first and second we have already examined (§§ 46, 47), and have only to note here the addition to the Clerk's Tale of the apostrophe, "O stormy peple, unsad and ever untrewe", and the ironical Envoy, "Grisild is deed and eek hir patience", introduced with the words, suspicious in the mouth of the Clerk, "and lat us stinte of ernestful matere"! Both additions are in Chaucer's strongest style, and were probably written about the year 1387, when he had lost his offices and belonged to the opposition to the party in power. The Franklin's Tale professes to be founded on an old Breton lay, of which no trace has yet been discovered. A similar story is told as the fifth of the tenth day in the *Decamerone*, but the differences of detail are too great for this to be the source on which Chaucer drew. As to the inverted morality of the tale, nothing need be added to what has been said already on Grisilde's acquiescence in the murder of her children. Husband and wife believe "Trouthe is the hyest thing that man may kepe", and to keep troth is regarded for the nonce as justifying all incidental sins. The tale (which is written in couplets) is easily and skilfully told, but is not in Chaucer's strongest style.

(iii.) From the tales of chivalry and nobility we may turn to the two legends of saints respectively assigned to the PRIORESS and the SECOND NUN. At the latter of these we have already looked (§ 45), and noted its comparative feebleness and prosaic adherence to its original. The Prioress's Tale, on the other hand, is, of its kind, as perfect as anything Chaucer ever wrote. Stories of little Christian boys murdered by the Jews for their devotion to the Blessed Virgin were common in the Middle Ages, and the theme is peculiarly suited to the tender-hearted Prioress to whom it is assigned. Three verses of the Prologue bear a strong resemblance to the Invocation to the Blessed Virgin which prefaces the Second Nun's Tale (*Lyf of Seint Cecyle*), and one of them is borrowed from the same passage in Dante. No exact original of the tale has been found, and it reads as if Chaucer were quite unfettered by any necessities of translation. Its beauty, its ideal suitability to the Prioress; the fact that the first verse of the Prologue, with its "quod she", was obviously written for her; the possible sly hit at the hunting Monk in the line "as monkes ben or elles oughten be"; the fact that "the murye wordes of the Hoste to Chaucer" which follow it are written in the same seven-line stanzas, whereas all the other talks in the *Tales* are in couplets— all these considerations tell strongly in favour of the story having been written expressly for its present place in the *Canterbury Tales* (*i.e.* probably about 1386), though so good a scholar as Professor Skeat was once content to assign it to the same date as the *Lyf of Seint Cecyle* (1373?) on the score of the similarity in subject and metre.

(iv.) Our last two "Gentles", the MONK and the DOC-TOUR OF PHYSIK, both go to history for their subjects. Of twelve of the Monk's tragedies we have already spoken (§ 48), the remaining five are concerned with Pedro of Spain (stabbed by his brother, 1369); Pedro of Cyprus (assassinated, also in 1369); Bernabo Visconti, Duke of Milan (died in prison, 1385); and Ugolino of Pisa (starved to death, with his children, in 1289). The second and third of these unfortunates are commemorated in only a stanza each; Pedro of Spain is allowed two stanzas, the second of which is interesting from its punning allusions; but it is the seven stanzas which tell of the death of Ugolino and his children that stand out from all the rest of the Monk's Tale. They are founded on the story in Dante's *Inferno*, canto xxxiii., but Chaucer has added something of his own, and the pathos of the whole is heartrending. Yet we may note his insistence on the tender age of the children (one of his additions) as a slight mark of weakness; Dante is content with writing "Ansel-muccio mio" (my little Anselm) instead of Anselmo. As to the Doctor's story of Appius and Virginia, this is rather poor work. It is an expansion to about four times its length of a passage of some seventy lines in the *Roman de la Rose*. The professed obligation to Livy is merely a translation of a line in the *Roman*, and, as Professor

Lounsbury has pointed out, it is inconceivable that Chaucer, if he had read Livy's pathetic story at first hand, should have spoilt it in the way he has. To make Virginius deliberately kill his daughter in cold blood, instead of in a sudden frenzy of despair, was a fatal mistake.

§ 74. **Tales of the Tradesfolk.**—The four Tales which we bring together under this heading, those of the SHIPMAN, WIFE OF BATH, MERCHANT, and MANCIPLE, are all marked by their license and lack of reticence, also by their shrewdness, knowledge of human nature (not at its highest), and sturdy middle-class independence. It is the Wife of Bath who delivers the fine speech on what makes a gentleman:

> But for ye speken of swich gentillesse
> As is descended out of old richesse,
> That therfore sholden ye be gentil-men,
> Swich arrogancè is nat worth an hen.
> Looke, who that is moost vertuous alway,
> Pryvee and apert, and moost entendeth ay
> To do the gentil dedès that he kan
> Take hym for the grettest gentil-man.
> Crist wol we clayme of hym oure gentillesse,
> Nat of oure eldres for hire old richesse.

It is the Manciple, again, who insists that the rich tyrant is no better than the poor thief. There is plenty of wisdom in all the talk about the goodness of good wives and the badness of bad ones, and the satire upon women is keen and yet not inhuman. The Manciple's Tale is built up on a story in Ovid's *Metamorphoses*; the sources of the other tales are not known, though parallels to them are not lacking. The morality of all of them is the morality of the *Decamerone* or the French *fabliaux*, but the digressions are mostly of more importance than the stories, and in these, as in the passage we have quoted from the Wife of Bath, we often have Chaucer at his best. As to the Wife's Prologue, it can only be said that the poet never wrote anything more masterly. It is the unblushing confession by a vulgar woman of her most intimate relations with her five husbands, and we can imagine that while it was in progress the Prioress rode a long way off. One incident may be recorded. The fifth husband, the Clerk Jankyn, had a library of invectives against women, and out of these— *Valerius* (*i.e.* Walter Map) *de non ducenda uxore,* Theophrastus *De Nuptiis,* St. Jerome "against Jovinian"—he used to read aloud, till one night the Wife tore three leaves out of his book, was so soundly beaten that she swooned away, and evermore ruled her repentant husband for his own good. Chaucer's remark on how different the books would have been if women had written them, shows that he had no great sympathy with Jankyn's favourite literature.

§ 75. **Tales of the Common Folk.**—(i.) We now come to the Tales of the MILLER who took triple toll, the REEVE who always got the better of his lord, the sleek intriguing FRIAR, the SOMPNOUR who winked at sin for a bottle of wine, and the COOK who was their fit comrade. Doubtless most of these rascals had some good in them, and a modern writer might suit them with sentimental stories which should leave us reflecting on the virtues of rogues and the prejudices of honest men. In the fourteenth century these refinements had not been invented. Churls they were, and churls' tales they told, says Chaucer, and if his readers dislike the stories they must turn the leaf and seek other ones. The plea is dramatically unassailable; but, to be honest, we must go a step farther. Clearly, Chaucer took a pleasure in telling these stories, and he told them marvellously well. The Reeve's Tale, one of the most monstrous of all, is perhaps the greatest artistic success, unsurpassed in all Chaucer's works for swiftness, vividness, and humour. To speak plainly, these churls' tales are all concerned with low tricks or downright sin. All that can be said for them is that they are told merrily and thoughtlessly, with no lingering over sin for its own sake, and with a general understanding that these things are done in the land of fiction. If we think of the actors in them as parishioners of the good Parson, whom it was his duty to turn into Christian men and women, the humour of the stories dies away, and there is little left but sordid tragedy. We may add that the plots seem to have been mostly taken from French or English popular stories, which Chaucer worked up in his own way.

(ii.) In three other tales, those of the PARDONER, NUN'S PRIEST, and CANON'S YEOMAN, Chaucer's mastery is hardly less, while his plots are of other kinds. Like the Wife of Bath, the Pardoner finds a safety-valve in a prologue, and his tale, of the three brothers who met Death in the form of a treasure over which they slew each other, is told with more sternness than we find elsewhere in Chaucer. In delightful contrast to this is the Priest's Tale, with its digressions on dreams and its banter between cock and hen. Two Italian stories and a Latin one have been found which offer parallels to the Pardoner's Tale, part of the plot of which is found also in Pāli! while that of the Priest's is based on an Æsopic fable which had been caught up into the *Roman de Renart*. For the Canon's Yeoman's story of the Alchemist no parallel even has been discovered, and it is written with so much insight into the tricks of those who professed their ability to multiply gold that Tyrwhitt imagined Chaucer to have recently had some personal dealings with these rascals. All three tales should be read as in the poet's best style.

§ 76. **Chaucer's own Tales.**—The talk before the Man of Law's Tale, which alludes to the *Legende of Good Women* as if the poet still hoped to complete it, is almost certainly earlier than "the murye wordes of the Hoste to Chaucer" which herald the *Tale of Sir Thopas*. We can hardly doubt that the Lawyer, who says distinctly "I speke in prose", was meant originally to tell the *Tale of Melibee*, which Chaucer later on humorously took upon himself after making Harry Bailey break off his parody of the romances. *Melibee* is a translation of a French version (perhaps by Jean de Meung) of the *Liber Consolationis et Consilii* of Albertano of Brescia. It is much more easily and pleasantly written than the *Boece*, but most modern readers will find the "noble wyf Prudence" a very dull orator. Of *Sir Thopas*, on the other hand, we would gladly have more. It is an example of the best kind of parody, which presents much of the charm of the original and yet is full of sly hits. The immense preparations and the small exploits, the "fair bearing" which lay in "drawing aback full fast" from the battle, the return to town as a prelude to resuming the fray, are all conceived in the most delightful vein of mock heroics, and we cannot quite forgive Harry Bailey his interruption. It is hardly necessary to point out the good taste of Chaucer's avoidance of reciting a serious poem in his own person in competition with those of his imaginary pilgrims.

§ 77. **The Parson's Tale and the Retractation.**—We may not leave the *Canterbury Tales* without dealing with two difficult questions. The Parson's sermon on penitence, as we have it, consists for the most part of a paraphrase of the *Somme de Vices et de Vertus* of Frère Lourens, a contemporary of Jean de Meung, in which the sacramental view of penitence and the need of confession to a priest, of penance and absolution, is duly upheld. The parts not translated from Frère Lourens are of a more evangelical character, and it has been maintained that these formed the first draft of the work, the long passages from the French being the additions of a clumsy interpolator. The sermon, as we have it, is ill-arranged, and contains enough illogicalities and contradictions to make

the theory of interpolation plausible. It is possible that
Chaucer showed his first draft to a friendly monk, who
pronounced it very incomplete, and was good-naturedly
bidden to set it right. It is even possible, as has been contended, that the sermon was rewritten after Chaucer's
death, in the interests of Catholic orthodoxy, or, as
we may prefer to say, of completeness. But this need
not make us believe either that the poet himself was a
Wycliffite, or that he meant his poor Parson to be a
Wycliffite, or that this supposed first draft was intended
as a Wycliffite sermon. Undoubtedly the *Canterbury
Tales* show the influence of Wyclif. Down to almost the
close of the theologian's life he had carried the common
sense of England with him, and shared with Chaucer the
patronage of John of Gaunt. Moreover, Wyclif's positive
teaching brought into the Church some of the new zeal
and life that come at times of reformation, heretical or
orthodox, and a country priest who had felt his influence
at Oxford would be likely to resemble closely Chaucer's
ideal parson. But all this is a very different matter from
maintaining that the poet followed the theologian in the
developments of the last few years of his life and consciously endeavoured to spread his doctrines; for this
supposition is contradicted by the whole tone and temper
of Chaucer's poetry.

The question of Chaucer's religious beliefs is raised again,
though in a different form, by the Retractation found at
the end of the *Canterbury Tales* in the best MSS. Here we
find written:

I biseke yow mekely for the mercy of God that ye preye for
me, that Crist have mercy on me and forgeve me my giltes: and
namely of my translacions and enditynges of worldly vanitees,
the whiche I revoke in my retraccions. As is the book of Troilus,
the book also of Fame, the book of the xxv. Ladies, the book of
the Duchesse, the book of Seint Valentynes day of the Parlement
of Briddes, the Tales of Canterbury, thilke that sownen into

synne, the book of the Leon and many another book if they were in my remembrance, and many a song and many a leccherous lay, that Crist for his grete mercy forgeve me the synne.

Only the *Boece* and his religious poems are excepted from condemnation. The incorrectness of the allusion to the *Legende* as the "book of the xxv. Ladies" throws some doubt on the genuineness of the Retractation, and many of Chaucer's lovers do not hesitate to pronounce this also a monkish invention. To the present writer it seems to have a genuine ring, nor does it appear contrary to human nature for the dying poet to stigmatise his works as "worldly vanitees" while abstaining, as far as we know, from any attempt to suppress them.

CHAPTER VII

LATER MINOR POEMS—CHAUCER'S RANK AS A POET

§ 78. "The Former Age" and "Fortune."—These two poems are both inserted in the best manuscript of Chaucer's *Boece* (Camb. MS. li. 3, 21). The first of them consists of eight stanzas of eight lines each, the last line of the seventh being unluckily wanting. The first four stanzas are founded on Boethius (Bk. ii. metre v.) and other hints are taken from the *Roman de la Rose*. The poem is a pleasant and ingenious composition on the old theme of the Golden Age. Far more important is the *Fortune* or *Balades de visage*[1] *sans peinture*, as it is called in the MSS., the "unpainted face" being that of the friend who is faithful in adversity. A strict ballade consists of three eight-line stanzas followed by a quatrain containing the envoy, usually addressed either to a prince or a lady. Only three rhymes are allowed, and the same line recurs at the end of each stanza, and of the envoy, to form the

---

[1] *Visage* is miswritten *vilage*.

refrain. In the *Fortune* Chaucer has given us a triple
ballade with a single envoy of seven lines (six in most
MSS.). The first ballade is entitled *Le Pleintif countre
Fortune,* and has as its refrain, "For fynally, Fortúne, I
thee defye". The second gives *le Respounse de Fortune au
Pleintif,* opening with the fine lines:

> No man is wrecched, but him-self it wene
> And he that hath him-self hath suffisaunce.

Fortune reminds the poet that he is born under her reign
of variance; she has taught him to know true friends from
false, but his anchor still holds, "and eek thou hast thy
beste frend alyve". The plaintiff replies and Fortune
again answers him, but in the end she takes up his cause,
and it is in her name that the envoy is written:

> Prynces, I prey yow of yowre gentilesse,
> Lat nat this man on me thus crye and pleyne,
> And I shall quyté yow yowre bysynesse
> At my requeste, as thre of yow or tweyne;
> And, but yow lest releve hym of hys peyne,
> Preyeth hys besté frend, of his noblesse,
> That to som beter estat he may atteyne.

Perhaps the fourth of these lines, omitted in all the
MSS. save one, should come after the fifth, nor can we
explain the allusions, either with it or without it, though
we may guess that the poem was written after Chaucer's
loss of office in December 1386. The character of Fortune
and some phrases are derived from the second book of the
De Consolatione, and Professor Skeat has shown that hints
are also taken from the *Roman de la Rose,* whose lines

> Je perdi trestous mes amis
> Fors ung—

may, indeed, be the foundation of the whole poem.

§ 79. "**Truth**", "**Gentilesse**", "**Lak of Stedfastnesse**".
—These three ballades strike a graver note than is common in Chaucer, and the first and second contain some

of his finest lines. All three are influenced or inspired by Boethius, but the *Truth* owes less to him than the others. All three also are written in seven-line stanzas, the first and third having envoys. The *Truth* is headed in one MS. *Balade de bon conseyl*. It opens with the magnificent line:

> Fle fro the pres and dwelle with sothfastnesse,

and contains the fine passage:

> Here is non home, here nys but wyldernesse.
> Forthe, pylgryme, forthe! forthe, beste, out of thi stal!
> Knowe thi contre, loke up, thonk God of al!
> Holde the heye weye, and lat thi gost thee lede,
> And trouthe shal delyver, it is no drede.

The last line forms the burden or refrain.

The *Gentilesse* has the same theme as the passage quoted from the Wife of Bath in § 74. Here we are taught:

> For unto vertue longeth dignytee
> And nought the révers, saufly dar I deme,
> Al were he mytre, croune, or dyademe.

The *Lak of Stedfastnesse*, a far inferior poem, laments the old days when "mannés word was obligacioun", and ends with the notable "envoy to King Richard":

> O prince, desire for to be honourable;
> Cherishe thi folke and hate extorcioun;
> Suffre no thing that may be reprevable
> To thyn estate doon in thi regyoune.
> Shewe forthe thy swerde of castigacioune;
> Drede God, do lawe, love trouthe and worthynesse,
> And drive thi folk agayn to stedfastnesse.

According to Shirley, the ballade was sent by Chaucer "to his souerain lorde kynge Rycharde the secounde, thane being in his Castell of Windesore". Professor Skeat and Dr. Koch assign it a date "between 1393 and 1399", but we cannot believe that Chaucer was remonstrating with Richard on his own misconduct. A more

likely date is May 1389, when the King declared that he
was old enough to govern for himself, and his rule was
welcomed as a relief to that of the Merciless Parliament
of 1388. The previous persecution of the royal Ministers
and the grant of £20,000 to the Lords Appellant seem
clearly alluded to in the lines:

> Pitee exiled, no wight is merciable.
> Through covetyse is blent discrescioun, etc.,

and it is probable that we may connect this address to
the King with the fresh period of prosperity which began
for Chaucer two months later. *Truth* and *Gentilesse* were
probably written a little earlier, *i.e.* while Chaucer was
still out of work.

§ 80. **"Treatise on the Astrolabe"—Last Poems.**—The
loss of his Clerkships in 1391 must have been a great blow
to Chaucer, and it is not unlikely that it checked the
stream of poetry which had been flowing from him so
ceaselessly during the last twelve years. Had his interest
in the *Canterbury Tales* still been keen, he would hardly
have turned aside to compose the prose TREATISE ON THE
ASTROLABE, which was probably his first work after his
loss of office. The astrolabe is a disc with complicated
figures on each side, useful for astrological calculations,
for reckoning the height of the sun, noting the positions
of stars, etc. Chaucer's treatise is mainly founded on
the *Compositio et Operatio Astrolabie* of Messahala, an
Arabian astronomer of the eighth century. It is very
useful in explaining the astronomical allusions in his own
poems, but its literary interest is almost confined to the
charming introduction addressed to "litell Lowys my
sone", for whom this treatise, prettily called "Bred and
mylk for childeren" in some MSS., was compiled. The
poet's vindication of his use of English, and his order to
his son to pray "God save the kyng, that is lord of this

langage, and alle that him feyth bereth and obeieth, euerech in his degree, the more and the lasse", are especially noteworthy.

About 1393–94 we find Chaucer at work at short poems —poems quite worthy of him, but now written with difficulty instead of ease.

> Ne thynke I never of slepe to wake my muse
> That rusteth in my shethe stille in pees,

he writes to Scogan, and in the envoy to his translation from Granson (see below) complains:

> For eld, that in my spirit dulleth me,
> Hath of endyting al the soteltee
> Wel nyghe bereft out of my remembraunce.

In defiance of the laws of love, Chaucer's friend, Henry Scogan, had confessed that "for his lady saw not his distress, therefore he gave her up at Michaelmess"—flat rebellion which caused all the country to be drenched with the tears of Venus, and for which he is here upbraided. But the sportive poem ends with a serious request that Scogan, who had influence at Windsor, would use it to help the poor Commissioner of the Greenwich roads (see §§ 18 and 38, 2), and the request seems to have borne fruit in the pension granted the next year. The poem is in seven seven-line stanzas, the envoy containing Chaucer's call upon his friend's kindness. Probably about the same time as this (see § 38, 2), Chaucer translated the three ballades of Sir Otes de Granson, to which the copyist Shirley gave the title THE COMPLEYNT OF VENUS, because both the originals and the translations were probably written to please Isabella of York, whom Shirley identified with the Venus of the *Compleynt of Mars* (§ 49). The French originals, traced at the end of the last century, show that Chaucer's version is fairly literal in the first two ballades but more free in the third. The envoy of ten lines (the three ballades are written in eight-line stanzas), with its complaint of old age and the scarcity of rhymes in English, is the best part of the poem, and this is Chaucer's own.

Some three years later, as is shown by the allusion to the prisoners in Friesland (§ 38, 2), Chaucer wrote his ENVOY TO BUKTON "touching marriage". This is a ballade in eight-line stanzas, and is full of bitter humour (or humorous bitterness, it is hard to say which) on the dotards who take on them the yoke of marriage when they might keep a free neck. Here also we may mention the two PROVERBS of four lines which have been attributed to Chaucer. If they are his, they show that the literary resurrectionist was abroad even in the fourteenth century, preserving trifles which their author would willingly have let die. Last of all, we have that humorously pitiful COMPLEYNT TO HIS EMPTY PURS, a ballade of seven-line stanzas, with a five-line envoy, in which, after bidding his purse "Beth hevy ageyn, or ellès mote I dye", the poet made his prayer to the "conquerour of Brutes Albioun", gaining thereby the additional pension which promised to shield him from penury during the rest of his life. None of these poems enhance Chaucer's reputation, but even these last drainings from his cup are all good wine.

§ 81. **Chaucer's Rank as a Poet.**—Now that we have examined piece by piece the whole of Chaucer's poetry, we must briefly consider the position which he occupies in English literature. General estimation rightly regards Shakespeare as our greatest poet, and places Milton on a pinnacle of lonely grandeur which makes comparison with him unprofitable. Next to Shakespeare, but far below him, we rank Chaucer. Far below him—because while Shakespeare had sounded life to its utmost depths and knew all its possibilities, Chaucer's knowledge of it was

only that of an acute man of the world. Next to him—
because Chaucer's shallower knowledge of life is yet
perfect of its kind, and is accompanied by an absolute
mastery of his art which (Milton being always excepted)
has never been equalled, save, perhaps, in a later day by
Lord Tennyson.

(i.) So far as his insight extended, Chaucer viewed life
from the same standpoint as Shakespeare. Their politics
were the same. Both honoured a true man in whatever
rank they found him; both detested the "many-headed
multitude", the "stormy peple, unsad and ever untrewe",
and had no fondness for the Jacks, whether Jack Straw
or Jack Cade, who put substantial well-to-do people in
fear for their lives and property. As to their religion, it is
curious to note that while Shakespeare lived in Protestant
times and is by many believed to have been a Roman
Catholic, Chaucer, who lived in Catholic times, has often
been claimed as a Protestant. The abuses of his time
caused the earlier poet to satirise the failings and sins
of the hangers-on of the Church, while Shakespeare's con-
servatism is mostly enlisted on the side of old observance.
But in each case we are sure that there is real religious
feeling in the background—a refuge to Chaucer from the
fleetingness of earthly pleasures, to Shakespeare from the
impenetrable mysteries of existence. The temper of both
men is sunny and tolerant, though we feel that the
serenity of Shakespeare's later plays rests on a deeper
foundation than Chaucer's cheery comradeship. But it is
in what they show us, that Chaucer's inferiority is most
manifest. He touches neither the height of passion nor
the depth of sorrow. The love of Troilus as compared with
the love of Romeo is as moonlight to sunlight. Tragedy
is to Chaucer only the falling from high estate; his pathos,
true and most touching so far as it goes, is hardly exercised save on a single theme—the anguish of a father or

mother when they see their children about to die and cannot help them.

(ii.) Thus, if we judge Chaucer only by his knowledge of the deeper side of life, a dozen English poets may claim to approach nearer to Shakespeare. But a poet must be judged firstly and mainly by his art; and as an artist, a master of his craft, Chaucer has no superior, not Shakespeare himself. The wonderful music in which a great thought finds expression in inevitable words came to him but seldom; but for sustained beauty, for continuous charm, his verse has never been surpassed. Alone among English poets he possesses the art of narration in its perfection. Save in one or two early poems, he is never for a moment dull, and he never cloys his readers with excess of sweetness. We feel that he is the most direct of story-tellers, and yet his narrative is never bald or thin; he has always ready at hand a touch of philosophy, a stroke of humour, or a vivid description, with which to keep up our interest and attention. His humour also has never been surpassed in its quaintness and subtlety. When can we be sure that we have exhausted it, or that beneath some seemingly simple phrase there is not waiting us a quiet jest? The vivid colour of his descriptions illumine Chaucer's pages with the brightness of a mediaeval manuscript. But of this most human, most lovable of English poets, it is idle, indeed, to try to summarise the just meed of praise.

APPENDIX

CHAUCER'S METRE AND VERSIFICATION—SPURIOUS AND DOUBTFUL WORKS

§ 82. **Chaucer's Metres.**—With the exception of the metrical experiments in *Anelida and Arcyte*, and the parody of the romance-metre in *Sir Thopas*, all Chaucer's poems are built up on eight (or nine) syllabled lines with four beats, or ten (or eleven) syllabled lines with five beats. The octosyllabic couplet he found in common use both in France and England, and employed it for his *Dethe of Blaunche* and *Hous of Fame*. The decasyllabic line appears in no less than twelve different arrangements: (1) the heroic couplet, used in the *Legende of Good Women* and most of the *Canterbury Tales*; (2) the five-line envoy to the *Compleynt to his Purs*, rhyming *aabba*; (3) the six six-line stanzas, all rhyming alike, *ababcb*, of the envoy to the Clerk's Tale; (4) his favourite seven-line stanza, called Rhyme-Royal from its subsequent use by James I. of Scotland, rhyming *ababbcc*, used in the *Pite*, *Parlement of Foules*, *Troilus*, four *Canterbury Tales*, etc.; (5) the eight-line stanza, rhyming *ababbcbc* of the *A B C*, Monk's Tale, *Former Age*, *Fortune*, and *Envoy to Bukton*; (6) a variety of this, imitated from Granson, in the *Compleynt of Venus*, rhyming *abab, bccb*; (7) a nine-line stanza, rhyming *aab aab; bcc*, in the *Compleynt of Mars*; also (8) a variety of this with only two rhymes, *aab, aab, bab*, in part of *Anelida*; (9) a ten-line stanza, rhyming *aab, aab, cddc*, in the *Compleynt to his Lady*; also (10) a variety of this with only two rhymes, *aab, aab, baab*, in the envoy of the *Compleynt of Venus*; (11) the roundel, rhyming *abb, ab*, ab, *baa*, abb (the roman letters mark the repeated lines), in the *Parlement of Foules* (cf. also the triple roundels of the *Merciles Beaute*, § 85); and (12) the *terza rima* of part of the *Compleynt to his Lady*. This last metre Chaucer imitated from Dante. To his decasyllabic stanza-metres parallels abound in contemporary French verse written under the influence of Machault; and in Machault also Professor Skeat has discovered an example of the heroic couplet, though for its elevation to the front rank among metres the English poet may claim exclusive credit. Moreover, Chaucer's handling of the different stanza-forms is distinctively his own, and his harmonies are more akin to those of the great Italian poets than to the slighter music of his French teachers.

It must be noted that whereas we have spoken of Chaucer's lines as octosyllabic and decasyllabic, most of them possess an additional unaccented syllable at the end, which gives a double (or feminine) rhyme instead of a single (or masculine)

one. If we take the first stanza of the Prologue to the Man
of Law's Tale as an example:

> O hateful harm! condicion of povertė
> With thurst, with coold, with hunger so confoundid!
> To asken help, thee shameth in thyn hertė.
> If thou noon aske, so soore artou y-woundid
> That verray nede unwrappeth al thy wounde hid;
> Maugre thyn heed, thou moste for indigencė
> Or stele, or begge, or borwe thy despencė—

the extra syllables at the end of the second, fourth, and fifth
lines cannot be mistaken, but they are equally present in
the others, and should be lightly sounded in reading aloud.

§ 83. **Variety and Smoothness of his Verse.**—Like every
other great poet, Chaucer was careful to vary his verse by
shifting the position of the pause or pauses, and with the
pause to help him, occasionally introduced an extra unaccented syllable in the middle of a line (*e.g. Blaunche*, l. 101,
"So whán this ládў̄/koude heére no wórd"). He also occasionally made a single long syllable supply the place of a long
and a short, or a short and a long, and sometimes does this
with very fine effect, as in *Blaunche*, ll. 126-128:

> And she, forwepėd and forwakėd
> Was werў̄; and thus the deed slepe
> Fíl/on her/or she/took kepe.

Or in *Pite*, l. 16:

> Adoun I fel, when that I saugh the herse,
> Deed/as stone,/whyl that/the swogh/me laste.

Or in such lines in the Prologue as:

> Al/bismot/red with his habergeon.—l. 76.
> Gin/glen in a whistlynge wynd als cleėre.—l. 170.
> "Púrs/is th' ercėdeknes helle," quod he.—l. 658.

Unfortunately he now and again makes some weak word,
like *in* or *that*, serve as a monosyllabic first foot (*e.g.* Prologue,
l. 391, "In/a gowne of faldyng to the knee"), and then the
temptation to emend is very great, though it should be
resisted. But as a general rule Chaucer's verse is perfectly
regular and perfectly smooth. The old complaints of its
roughness were founded partly on the habit of his early

editors of omitting from every second or third line some such little word as *that, to, the, for, in,* and the like; partly on the general carelessness and ignorance as to pronunciation of the *e* final, which plays so large a part in his verse. This *e* final is to be sounded when it represents the old vowel termination of a noun in Anglo-Saxon, even sometimes when the vowel termination properly belonged only to the oblique cases of the old inflection. In nouns of French origin it is mostly sounded, but not always. It is to be sounded when it represents the dative case of monosyllabic nouns, or the definite form or the plural of monosyllabic adjectives, or the subjunctive or infinitive of verbs, or (in the case of strong verbs) the past participle; also as an adverbial termination. On the other hand, it is usually elided before a vowel and before some of the commonest words beginning with *h,* and is specially liable to be silent after *r.* Complete rules on this subject will be found in *Chaucer's Sprache und Verskunst,* by Professor Bernhard Ten Brink, and in many less elaborate works.

§ 84. **Chaucer's Nicety as to Rhymes.**—Chaucer's fine sense of harmony is peculiarly evident in the nicety of his rhymes. In *Troilus* ii. 884-6-7, he has made *syke* rhyme with *endite* and *white,* and this is the only assonance in place of a full rhyme for which he is responsible in all his works. Again, however lightly the final *e* may have been pronounced at the end of a line, this light sound was enough to make him rigorously avoid rhyming any word to which it belonged with one to which it did not belong. Thus, there is only one doubtful instance in all his works in which he rhymes a word properly ending in *-i* or *-y* with one properly ending in *-ie* or *-ye.*[1] He never makes an adverb like *synfully, tenderly, trewely,* etc., rhyme with a substantive of French origin like *chivalrye, curteisye, glotonye,* or with infinitives like *crye, espye, gye.* The same carefulness is shown in the avoidance of all other rhymes which would link together words which, for any of the reasons given in the previous section, can claim an *e* final, with those to which it does

[1] In Squire's Tale, l. 503, *sky* rhymes with *by*; in *Hous of Fame* (Bk. iii. l. 501), *skye* rhymes with *hye* (adv. of *high*); but there is a slight difference of meaning sufficient to make *sky* and *skye* different words.

not properly belong. Rhymes such as *dighte* (inf.) with *delit* (subst.), as *al* (adv.) with *falle* (inf.), as *solas* with *grace*, were impossible to Chaucer. Special cases of this objection to false *e* rhymes are his refusal to rhyme (i.) an infinitive with the singular of a strong preterite indicative; (ii.) an infinitive with a weak perfect participle; and (iii.) a strong preterite with a weak one. He objects also to rhyming a weak perfect participle (except it be the plural of a monosyllabic one) with a weak preterite; but from this objection he departs in fourteen cases in his 35,000 lines, so that it cannot be elevated into a rigid rule.

§ 85. **Application of the Rhyme Test to Poems ascribed to Chaucer.**—A poet who throughout the 35,000 lines of his undoubted work has shown the most delicate apprehension of even slight differences in sound cannot be lightly credited with poems in which these differences are ignored. Hence Chaucer's practice in regard to rhyme, as sketched in the preceding section, affords a ready test with which to try the authenticity of the numerous works which have been assigned to him. The history of his text can be very briefly stated. Of the twenty-five works shown to be Chaucer's in the Table on p. 38, no less than nineteen (together with the *Romaunt of the Rose*) were printed in Thynne's edition of 1532; the *Proverbs, Compleynt to his Lady*, and *Adam Scrivener* were added by Stow in 1561; the *A B C* by Speght in 1602; the *Former Age* (discovered by Henry Bradshaw) by Dr. Morris in 1875; the *Rosemounde* by Professor Skeat in 1891. Over against these twenty-five undoubted poems we have no less than fifty others, mostly short, but containing altogether some 17,000 lines, which the complaisance of various editors has from time to time stamped with Chaucer's name. These fifty poems fall into two divisions: (*a*) the forty-three which were added by Thynne, Stow, Speght, and Urry; and (*b*) the little handful of seven which have been assigned to Chaucer without certain evidence in modern times.

Lists of the forty-three works habitually printed with Chaucer's in the sixteenth and seventeenth centuries will be found in Professor Skeat's *The Chaucer Canon* (1900), in Professor Lounsbury's *Studies in Chaucer*, vol. i. (1891), and in Eleanor Prescott Hammond's *Chaucer: a bibliographical manual* (New York, 1908). Long before increased grammatical knowledge had made the rhyme tests possible, the ascription of most of these poems to Chaucer was felt to be absurd. Some of them are avowed continuations or imitations of his genuine works; of others, the real authors—Lydgate, Hoccleve, and Robert Henryson—were easily discovered; others again were palpably later, or not in his style. Only five of these poems survived the analysis of Thomas Tyrwhitt—the first editor who brought a critical judgment to bear upon Chaucer, though unfortunately his work only extended to the *Canterbury Tales*, which he published in 1775–78. These five poems are the *Complaint of the Black Knight*, which we now know, on Shirley's authority, to be by Lydgate; the *Cuckoo and the Nightingale*, a pretty poem in stanzas rhyming *aabba*, which begins with two lines quoted from the Knight's Tale, and is now known to be by (Sir Thomas?) Clanvowe; and the *Court of Love, Isle of Ladies*, and the *Flower and the Leaf* (the last avowedly the work of a woman), all of them in language later (in the case of the *Court of Love* much later) than that of Chaucer, and all transgressing his rules as to rhyme. In 1897 Skeat added to his edition of Chaucer's *Complete Works* a seventh volume entitled *Chaucerian and other Pieces*, containing twenty-nine of the more notable accretions which he had rejected from his text, the only notable omission being *The Isle of Ladies* (also known as *Chaucer's Dream*), which had to be omitted on account of its length. Here may be found *The Testament of Love*, by Thomas Usk (prose), *The Plowman's Tale* (avowedly not by Chaucer), poems known to be by Gower, Hoccleve (2), Scogan and Lydgate (10), *La Belle Dame sans Mercy* by Sir Richard Ros, Henryson's *The Testament of Creseide*, Clanvowe's *Cuckoo and the Nightingale*, *The Flower and the Leaf* and *The Assembly of Ladies* (both by a woman), and *The Court of Love*, with six shorter pieces. Of the anonymous poems, only *The Flower and the Leaf* takes high rank.

The only original poems as to which there is now any controversy are seven short pieces discovered or rediscovered by Skeat and printed by him in his great edition—two, numbered xi. and xii., in his text; three (xxi.-xxiii.) at the end of his first volume, with the prefatory note, "The following poems are probably genuine, but are placed here for lack of external evidence"; and three others (xxiv.-xxvi.) which follow the introduction to his fourth volume. Of these, xi. (*To Rosemounde*) has been generally accepted (see § 5), though Professor Brusendorff objects, and xii. (*Merciles Beaute*), xxi. (*Ageynst Women Unconstant*, also called *Newfangleness*), xxii. (*An Amorous Compleynt* or *Compleynt d'Amours*), xxiii. (*A Balade of Compleynt*), xxiv. (*Balade that Chaucier made* or *Womanly Noblesse*) received various degrees of support and were admitted by Sir Frank Heath to an Appendix to his text of the Minor Poems in the *Globe Chaucer*. On the other hand, xxv. and xxvi. (*Compleint to my Mortal Foe* and *Compleint to my Lodesterre*) met with little or no support. In supporting Chaucer's authorship to these poems, Skeat relied on their poetical quality, their compliance with Chaucer's practice as regards purity of rhyming, their imitation (in some cases) of French authors whom Chaucer imitated, and their occurrence in manuscripts along with poems undoubtedly Chaucer's. None of these considerations has any compelling force, and their acceptance involves a belief that there was no one besides Chaucer at the court of Richard II. capable of writing even moderately good short poems, in which, because they are short, the observance of the rhyme tests does not count for very much. Some of these poems, notably *Merciles Beaute*, first claimed for Chaucer by Bishop Percy in 1765 on the ground of its following some of his undoubted poems in Pepys MS. 2006, are very charming; but it is not worth while even for these to disturb the strength of the Chaucer canon, which at present rests exclusively on the authority of the poet himself, or of manuscripts written shortly after his death.

   § 86. **The Romaunt of the Rose.**—This satisfactory condition of the Chaucer canon is only disturbed by one vexed question, the propriety of ascribing to Chaucer any part of the existing fragmentary translation of the *Roman de la Rose*. We know from himself that Chaucer did translate this work, but, as it was immensely popular, this by no means proves that the extant translation, first ascribed to him in 1532, was the one he made. The evidence, indeed, at first sight is all the other way. Judged as a whole, the extant translation appears distinctly un-Chaucerian. It contains a considerable admixture of northern forms in positions where they are essential to the rhyme, and therefore cannot be due to the copyist. It contains a small percentage of assonances in place of true rhymes. It also violates repeatedly the rhyme tests by rhyming -*y* with -*ye*, and words or forms to which the *e* final is essential with other words or forms which have no claim to it. Either, then, we must believe that, at one period of his life, Chaucer used northern forms, assonances, and rhymes which in all his other poems he rejects, or we must give up Chaucer's authorship of the extant text as a whole. An explanation of the northern forms has been sought for in Chaucer's probable winter residences in Yorkshire while in the service of the Countess of Ulster, but this suggestion only accounts for Chaucer's knowledge of northern English, not for his use of northern forms in a single poem out of all his works. A gallant attempt to counterbalance the evidence of the rhymes, by producing a number of small phrases or catchwords which were used in about the same proportion in the *Romaunt* as by Chaucer, has also failed, for the same phrases have been found abundantly in other works. Meanwhile, however, it has been noted that the first 1705 lines of the *Romaunt*, though not absolutely free from bad rhymes, are strikingly more correct in this respect than the rest of the translation. It has been proposed, therefore, to assign these first 1705 lines to Chaucer, and the rest of the version to another hand, or rather to two other hands, B being made responsible for ll. 1706-5810, and C for ll. 5811 to end. The difficulties in the way of accepting this theory are (i.) that Chaucer distinctly says his translation was a "heresy against Love's law", a phrase more applicable to the later portion by Jean de Meung than to ll. 1-1705, *i.e.* we must suppose that he translated beyond this point, but that his translation is lost; (ii.) that judged by merely literary tests there is no sufficient break at l. 1705 to allow us to believe that we have here two distinct translations pieced together by a scribe. We are asked, therefore, to believe that the rest of Chaucer's version was lost within a few years of its being made, and its place supplied by a skilful continuator, who caught up the tone of Chaucer's translation, though he could not free himself from his own dialect and false rhymes. A theory which would make Chaucer the author of the whole translation in his youth, and its reviser up to l. 1705 when his language and versification were more educated, does not seem exposed to more difficulties than that of his authorship of ll. 1-1705 only. Yet another explanation put forward by Professor Aage Brusendorff (*The Chaucer Tradition*, 1925) is that a northern reciter started to set down on paper what he could remember of Chaucer's version, began to supplement his memory by botching soon after l. 1705, and got steadily worse until at l. 5810 he broke off, skipped some thousands of lines, and then went on for another 1900 lines with fair success till he came to a stop. This accounts, rather attractively, for the facts, but is hardly susceptible of proof.

§ 87. **The Pourtrayal of Living Persons in the Canterbury Pilgrims.**—As already mentioned in § 61, Professor Manly, in his *Some New Light on Chaucer* (1926), suggested that since Harry Bailey, the Southwark innkeeper, is certainly, and Oswald, the reeve of Baldeswell, almost certainly, a real person, we may look to find other real persons among the pilgrims, or at least details, mostly satirical, in the descriptions, which would make anyone familiar with London and the Court promptly guess from whom they were taken. In considering this suggestion we must remember that the *Canterbury Tales* never attained any such approach to completeness as would have led to their being "published", even in the limited sense in which *Troilus* and the *Boece* may have been published, *i.e.* by a scrivener being allowed to make copies of them for sale, in return perhaps for having made earlier copies for Chaucer to offer to his patrons. On the other hand, in the *Envoy à Bukton*, Chaucer bids his friend to "read" the "Wife of Bath", and we must thus believe that, as the tales (and in some cases the talks on the road) were written, copies were made which were passed round among the poet's friends. In manuscripts circulating in this way Chaucer could write harmlessly about the Host of the Tabard and even let his real name slip out in one of the Talks, though if he was the Henricus Baylley who in 1376-77 and

1378–79 represented Southwark in Parliament he was a man
of some importance. As for Oswald, the reeve of Baldeswell
in Norfolk, he would never hear of poems circulated privately
at Court; and on the other hand, if the "rekenyng" which he
had given "syn that his lord was twenty yeer of age" related to the estates of John Hastings, second Earl of Pembroke (who left England soon after coming of age in 1368
and never returned, dying abroad in 1375), one of Chaucer's
friends, Sir William de Beauchamp, would have been pleased
at the aspersions on the Reeve's honesty, for Beauchamp
had been superseded as one of the trustees of Pembroke's
estate by the Countess of Norfolk, who was already managing
another section of it in which Baldeswell lay. So again
Prof. Manly offers reasons for identifying the Sergeant-atte-
lawe, of whom Chaucer wrote "ther koudė no wight pynche
at his writyng", with Thomas Pynchbek, a Sergeant who
became Chief Baron of the Exchequer in 1388 and had
annoyed Beauchamp by treating contemptuously claims he
believed he had to Pembroke's estates. Prof. Manly has also
found bits of evidence for connecting the Franklin with
Sir John Bussy or Bushy, one of Richard II.'s favourites,
and thinks that the Shipman may have been modelled on
John Hawley, one of the boldest of the piratical seamen of
Dartmouth in Chaucer's time. These suggestions may be
strengthened and extended by further researches. As new
discoveries such possible borrowings of touches from real
persons are of great interest, but it seems probable that, even
if Prof. Manly's suggestions are confirmed, Chaucer only
amused himself and his friends by a little personal satire as
a byplay to his great work. We are in no way invited to
think of the Man of Law's Tale of Constance, not very appropriate to any lawyer, being in any way specially appropriate to Sergeant Pynchbek, or his prefatory remarks as
made by the Sergeant. Most imaginary portraits have owed
something to hints taken from real persons, and they are not
necessarily any less universal in their interest and import.

THE END